with contributions by
William Richardson

Do It!

Play and Teach Trombone

A Musical Text for Secondary Instrument Courses with a "Focus on Teaching"

James O. Froseth

Molly A. Weaver, Contributing Editor

Instrument	Book and CD
Woodwind	
Flute	M587
Clarinet	M588
Oboe	M589
Bassoon	M590
Alto Sax	M591
Woodwind Teacher's Edition	M592
Brass	
Trumpet	M595
Horn in F	M596
Trombone	M597
Euphonium/Baritone	M598
Tuba	M599
Brass Teacher's Edition	M600

Index to "FOCUS ON TEACHING"

GETTING IT "RIGHT" FROM THE START
Table of Contents

GETTING IT "RIGHT" FROM THE START
CD Index

Index to Music Repertoire

Index to Supplementary Resources

GOALS AND OBJECTIVES

Trombone Home Helper has two primary goals: 1) to provide students with the home help needed to develop exemplary performance habits and practice procedures from the start, and 2) to transform early success playing the trombone into a lifetime of musical enjoyment and participation.

Objective 1:
To exhibit all the performance skills represented by the player in the photograph.

Step 1:
Look carefully at the photograph to develop a mental image of the physical set-up you will need to be a successful trombone player.

Objective 2:
To sound as much like the player on the CD as possible.

Step 2:
Listen to Track 1 on your *Play and Teach* CD to develop an overall concept of the task you are about to undertake.

FOCUS ON TEACHING

You Know You Are Prepared to Teach When You Are Able to:

- **Predict** exactly what you want to see and hear at the conclusion of every lesson or rehearsal

- **Discriminate** differences between what you are predicting and what you are seeing and hearing during each lesson or rehearsal

- **Remediate** deficiencies that you see and hear

   Note: Abilities to predict expected outcomes, discriminate differences, and remediate deficiencies represent teaching skill and lesson planning at the highest level.

Suggestion: Employ the *Visual Diagnostic Skills Program* for Brass (M-536) and Woodwinds (M-537) to develop your abilities to visually predict, discriminate, and remediate. www.giamusic.com

Suggestion: Employ the artist models on *Do It! Play and Teach* CDs to develop your abilities to aurally predict, discriminate, and remediate.

KEYS TO SUCCESS

STUDENT – You will be much more likely to succeed if you:

1) take proper care of your instrument,
2) read every word of the text and follow all instructions,
3) practice with the CD every day,
4) follow the lead of your teacher, and
5) attend every lesson at school equipped to play and prepared to learn.

HOME HELPER – You will be most helpful to your student if you:

1) help your student to take proper care of the instrument,
2) read every word of the text,
3) monitor practice sessions regularly,
4) encourage your student to practice with the CD every day,
5) check off each achievement on every CHECKLIST once each week (remember, every check is a motivating "pat on the back"),
6) avoid negative comments,
7) give your student lots of attention, and
8) communicate with the teacher through your *Home Helper* book when questions or concerns arise.

TEACHER – You will be most helpful to your student if you:

1) recognize and record student achievement, and
2) coordinate the home helper's efforts with school instruction.

FOCUS ON TEACHING

What Are the Predictors of Music Achievement Prior to the Start of Instruction?

- Past achievement is the best predictor of future achievement.
- Students who move well to music are more likely to be successful instrumentalists than students who do not.
- Students who sing well are more likely to be successful instrumentalists than students who do not.
- Students who have learned to play an instrument such as recorder, piano, or guitar are more likely to be successful instrumentalists than students who do not.

What Are the Predictors of Music Achievement After the Start of Instruction?

- Physical compatibility with the chosen instrument
- Quality of instrument
- Quality of instruction
- Opportunities to pursue self-determined musical interests
- Self-motivation
- Home help

CARE OF THE TROMBONE

Your trombone is a fragile instrument that requires special care. Satisfactory musical progress is possible only if your instrument is in proper playing condition. Be especially careful of your slide. Sit back far enough from the people in front of you to avoid hitting them or their chairs. Put your stand up high enough to avoid hitting it with the top of your slide. Sit to the left of your stand whenever possible. Allow ample space behind you also. If anything should go wrong with your trombone, DO NOT ATTEMPT YOUR OWN REPAIRS. Only a qualified repair person has the experience and skill to service your trombone. If you need advice, consult your teacher or your music dealer.

Proper instrument care begins with clean teeth and clean hands. Always brush your teeth after eating to avoid blowing food particles into your instrument. If you are unable to brush, rinse your mouth with water before playing. To protect the finish on your trombone, wash your hands before playing and use a soft cloth to wipe off your instrument after playing.

Keep your trombone in its case when you are not playing it to avoid damage and costly repairs. Always secure the latches immediately after you close the lid. Do not force books, music, CDs, or other items into the case on top of the trombone or beside it. Avoid exposing your instrument to extreme heat or cold, moisture or excessive humidity, sharp blows, dirt, or other possible sources of damage.

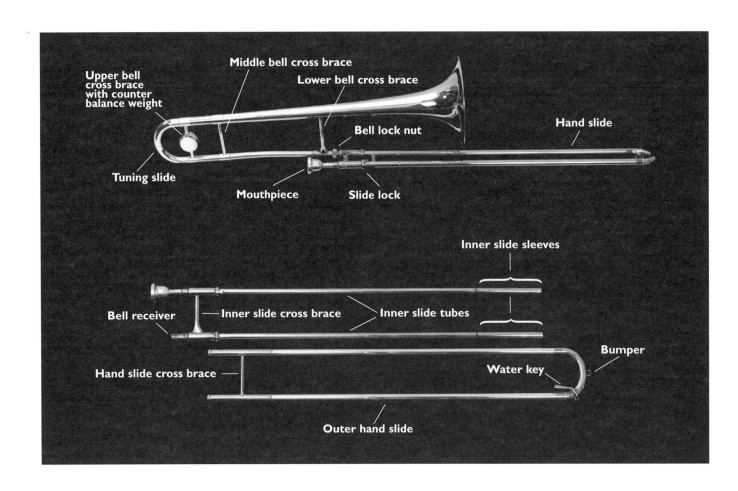

GUIDELINES FOR PRODUCTIVE PRACTICE

Guiding principle: Practice must have purpose.

Step 1. Decide what it is you want to accomplish. For example:

1. **"I want to improve my:"**
   A. Embouchure (pages 8, 9, 10, and 11).
   B. Posture and Instrument Position (page 14).
   C. Left Hand Position (page 15).
   D. Right Hand Position (page 16).

2. **"I want to sound more like the model on the CD when I play on my mouthpiece."**
   (Tracks 2, 3, and 4 on pages 8 and 11)

3. **"I want to improve my ability to play higher and lower on my mouthpiece."** (Tracks 5 and 6 on page 11)

4. **"I want to improve my articulation."** (Tracks 8 and 9 on page 13)

5. **"I want to improve my ability to listen and play what I hear."**
   (Tracks 10, 11, 12, 13, 14, 15, and 16 on pages 19, 20, 21, and 22)

6. **"I want to sound more like the player on the CD when I play *Practice Every Day March*."**
   (Track 1 on page 20)

7. **"I want to breathe and phrase more like the player on the CD."** (Track 1 on page 20)

RECOMMENDATIONS

1. Schedule several short practice sessions daily rather than one extended session.

2. Take frequent breaks during practice sessions to avoid fatigue.

3. Be spontaneous. Practice whenever you feel motivated to make music or improve your performance skills.

4. Encourage your adult home helper to oversee your practice as often as possible.

5. Schedule a regular weekly session for your adult home helper to enter achievement marks on every CHECKLIST.

FOCUS ON TEACHING
A Strategy for Teaching Music Performance

- Determine the Need for Instruction
  - New Material
  - Deficiencies Revealed through Ongoing Assessment of Student Performance
    Teacher Assessment
    Self-Assessment
    Peer Assessment
    Adult Home Helper Assessment

- Show Students the Specific Objective
  "It Sounds Like"
  "It Looks Like"

- Teach to the Objective
  - New Material: Teach and Evaluate the Effects of Instruction
  - Deficiencies Revealed through Assessment: Remediate and Evaluate the Effects of Remedial Instruction

Suggestion: Regularly employ *Band Home Helper* photographs and CD artist models to direct students' attention to specific music performance objectives. www.giamusic.com

POSTURE

Correct posture is an essential element of instrumental performance. With correct posture you will be able to develop proper breathing, breath control, and playing position.

Step 1: Sit forward on the edge of the chair with the weight of your upper body slightly forward.

Step 2: Sit with a straight back and erect head.

Step 3: Position both feet flat on the floor.

Note: You should feel well balanced and free of tension.

Step 4: Demonstrate that you have proper posture by standing without having to shift your upper body weight forward.

MARK ✔ or ? HERE			
Week			
Step			
1	2	3	4
5	6	7	8

1			

2			

3			

4			

FOCUS ON TEACHING
Positive Teaching versus Negative Teaching

- A positive instructional statement defines the objective and focuses the student's attention on the desired behavior.

  "Now, do what I do. Sit up, straight, forward on the edge of the chair."

- A negative instructional statement does not define the objective nor does it focus the student's attention on the desired behavior.

  "Don't slouch."

Suggestion: Use the positive models and descriptions in *Trombone Home Helper* to focus students' attention on desired performance behavior. www.giamusic.com

BREATHING AND BREATH CONTROL EXPERIMENTS

EXPERIMENT 1: Learning about the Expansion and Contraction of the Abdominal Area

Step 1: Sit on the edge of your chair, bend over, and place your elbows on your knees;

Step 2: Inhale a full breath of air very quickly through your mouth (as you would gasp if you suddenly stepped into an ice-cold shower);

Step 3: Hold your breath and note how your back and abdominal area has been expanded by the air in your lungs;

Step 4: Quickly exhale all the air in your lungs with a hissing sound;

Step 5: Note how your back and abdominal area has been contracted by the release of the air from your lungs;

Step 6: Sit up straight, place the thumbs and fingers of both hands around your body at the lowest rib, and repeat Steps 2, 3, 4, and 5.

EXPERIMENT 2: Learning about Sustaining the Airstream

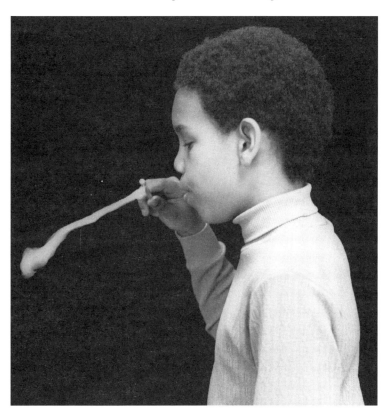

Step 1: Tape a 3/8-inch by 7-inch strip of facial tissue to an ordinary pencil at a right angle;

Step 2: Hold the pencil parallel to the floor and approximately three inches directly in front of your mouth;

Step 3: Inhale a full breath of air quickly through your mouth;

Step 4: Exhale a concentrated stream of air through a small opening in your lips so as to blow the strip of tissue out at an angle toward the floor;

Step 5: Sustain the stream of air to hold the tissue out for at least 5 to 10 seconds.

Suggestion: Keep a record of how long you can hold the tissue out with your airstream. Try to increase your time a little each day.

FOCUS ON TEACHING

The Orchestration of Experience as a Teaching Strategy

• A learning experience will almost always produce a better result than descriptive teacher-talk.

Note: Telling a student to breath from the diaphragm is not particularly helpful because there is no other way to breathe.

Suggestion: Employ the breathing and breath control experiments above to allow students to experience full diaphragmatic breathing.

FIRST TONES ON THE MOUTHPIECE

TRY THIS FIRST

• SOUNDS LIKE:

CD Track 2 *LISTEN TO THE CD and BUZZ*

| Listen
to the CD | Buzz | Buzz Along
with the CD | Listen
to the CD | Buzz | Buzz Along
with the CD |

• LOOKS LIKE:

Many students will form an acceptable embouchure with a simple photographic representation of the embouchure and a recorded model of the sound made by buzzing on the mouthpiece.

Too much verbal information can confuse your student and lead to mental overload.

To assess your student's embouchure refer to page 9 for a checklist of physical characteristics that define an acceptable trombone embouchure.

To take your student through a step-by-step formation of the embouchure turn to page 10.

FOCUS ON TEACHING

Helping Students Make the Best Choice of Instrument

- Every student has unique physical characteristics.
- Some students have physical characteristics that are not well suited to their first choice of instrument.
- Finding the best physical match can be the difference between success and failure.

Suggested Procedure: Use the photographs, CD sound tracks, and suggested procedures contained in "Choosing for Success," *Teacher's Reference and Resource Edition, Home Helper for Band* to aid students in making the best choice of instrument. www.giamusic.com

KEY ELEMENTS OF THE TROMBONE EMBOUCHURE

The word "embouchure" (ahm-bu-shure) refers to the position and use of the lips and facial muscles to produce a tone on a wind instrument.

✔ **If Satisfactory**   ❓ **If More Work Is Needed**

A. The corners of the mouth are firm and puckered inward toward the center of the mouth.

Note: The upper and lower teeth should be slightly apart and approximately aligned.

Note: A natural alignment of the teeth should position the mouthpiece at a slightly downward angle.

B. The chin muscles are drawn downward.

C. A concavity is visible between the lower lip and chin.

D. The mouthpiece is positioned to the center of the mouth with 2/3 upper lip and 1/3 lower lip within the rim of the mouthpiece.

Note: Variations resulting from an unusual shape of the lips, formation of the teeth, or jaw structure are acceptable. Mouthpiece placement of approximately 1/2 upper lip and 1/2 lower lip may also be acceptable.

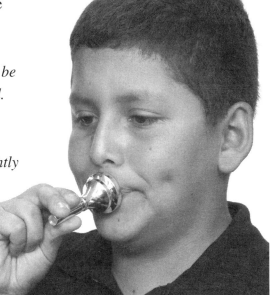

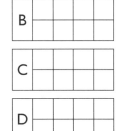

	MARK ✔ or ❓ HERE			
	Week			
Step	1	2	3	4
	5	6	7	8
A				

B			
C			
D			

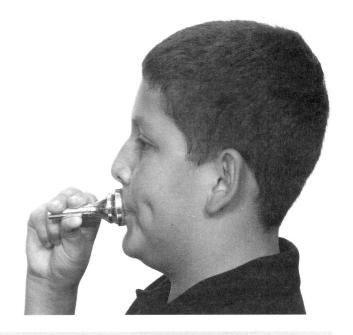

FOCUS ON TEACHING

It "Sounds Right" But It Doesn't "Look Right"

• Owing to the wide range of physical characteristics among instrumental students, it may not be possible to achieve the "right look" in every case.

• "Sounds right" should overrule "looks right" unless an unusual physical set-up has the potential to compromise the long-term development of range and endurance.

FORMING THE TROMBONE EMBOUCHURE - STEP-BY-STEP

Step 1: Bring your lips together by pronouncing the syllable "em."

Note: Your upper and lower teeth should be slightly apart and approximately aligned.

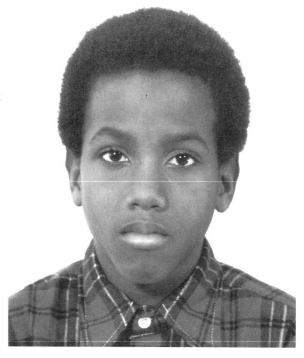

MARK ✔ or ? HERE				
	Week			
Step	1	2	3	4
	5	6	7	8
1				

Step 2: Firm the corners of your mouth and draw your chin muscles downward to form a concavity between your lower lip and chin.

Note: Keep the corners of your mouth focused firmly inward to prevent puffy lips or cheeks.

Note: Keep your lower jaw in the "em" position as you draw your chin muscles downward.

2			

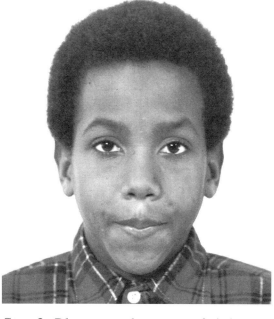

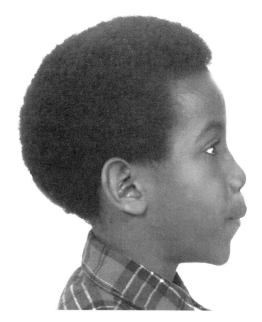

Step 3: Blow a steady stream of air between your lips to make a long buzzing sound.

Note: The opening between your vibrating lips is called the "aperture."

3			

Step 4: If your lips fail to buzz after several attempts, continue on to page 11. Return to this checklist after you learn to buzz your mouthpiece.

4			

PLACING THE MOUTHPIECE ON THE LIPS

Step 1: Bring your lips together to form the syllable "em."

Step 2: Firm the corners of your mouth inward toward the center of your mouth.

Step 3: Draw your chin muscles downward.

Step 4: Position the mouthpiece to the center of your lips with 2/3 upper lip and 1/3 lower lip within the rim of the mouthpiece.

Note: Variations resulting from an unusual shape of the lips, formation of the teeth, or jaw structure are acceptable. Mouthpiece placement of approximately 1/2 upper lip and 1/2 lower lip may also be acceptable.

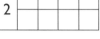

MARK ✔ or ? HERE

Step	Week			
	1	2	3	4
	5	6	7	8

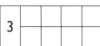

1				

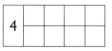

2				

3				

4				

PLAYING ON THE MOUTHPIECE

Step 1: Position the mouthpiece and take a full breath of air in through your mouth.

Caution: Inhaling through your nose will prevent you from taking in a full breath of air.

Step 2: Form the embouchure and make a long buzzing sound by blowing a steady stream of air into the mouthpiece.

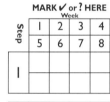

MARK ✔ or ? HERE

Step	Week			
	1	2	3	4
	5	6	7	8

1				

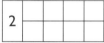

2				

LISTEN TO THE CD and PLAY

CD Track 2

Listen to the CD	Play	Play Along with the CD

CD Track 3

Listen to the CD	Play	Play Along with the CD

CD Track 4

Listen to the CD	Play	Play Along with the CD

PLAYING HIGHER AND LOWER ON THE MOUTHPIECE

LISTEN TO THE CD and PLAY HIGHER and LOWER

CD Track 5

Listen to the CD	Play	Play Along with the CD

CD Track 6

Listen to the CD	Play	Play Along with the CD

MUSICAL ARTICULATION

Articulation refers to how the tone is started and how it is stopped. This important aspect of instrumental performance requires correct posture, correct breathing and breath control, and a good embouchure.

Starting the Tone

A tone is started when a stream of air from the lungs sets the lips vibrating. The tongue acts as the valve that releases the airstream into the mouthpiece. Figure 1 below shows the position of the tongue against the upper front teeth where they meet the gums prior to the start of the tone. Figure 2 illustrates the position of the tongue after the tone has begun. *NOTE: The lower jaw remains stable while tonguing.*

Stopping the Tone

There are two acceptable ways to stop a tone. The first is by stopping the airstream. This method is used at the end of a long tone, before a silence in the music, and for separated styles of articulation. Pronounce the syllables "tu," "tu," "tu," "tu," with a space after each syllable to simulate this style of articulation. The second way to stop the tone is by simply touching the upper teeth where they meet the gums quickly and lightly with the tongue. This method is used for fast tonguing and for a connected style of articulation. To simulate this style of articulation pronounce the syllables "du–du–du–du–" with the sensation that the airflow is continuous. Avoid articulation that sounds like the syllables "thu," "hu," "thut," or "hutt."

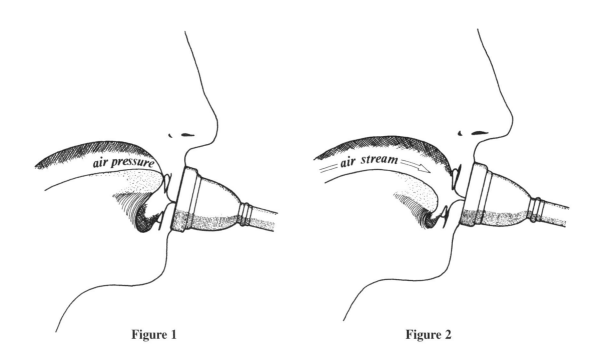

Figure 1   **Figure 2**

MUSICAL ARTICULATION ON THE MOUTHPIECE

Step 1: Position the mouthpiece on your lips.

Step 2: Inhale a full breath of air through your mouth.

Caution: Inhaling through your nose will prevent you from taking a full breath of air.

Step 3: Form your embouchure, blow, and release your tongue as though pronouncing the syllable "tu."

Step 4: Demonstrate the separated style of articulation with the syllable "tu."

Note: Keep your lower jaw and embouchure still while tonguing.

Step 5: Demonstrate the connected style of articulation with the syllable "du."

Note: Keep your lower jaw and embouchure still while tonguing.

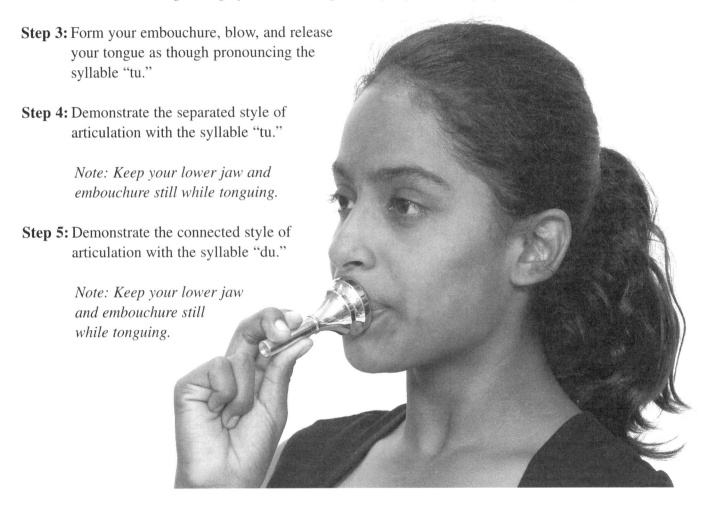

CD Track 7 *MUSICAL ARTICULATION - JUST LISTEN*

THE SEPARATED STYLE OF ARTICULATION

CD Track 8 *LISTEN TO THE CD and PLAY*

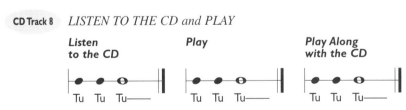

THE CONNECTED STYLE OF ARTICULATION

CD Track 9 *LISTEN TO THE CD and PLAY*

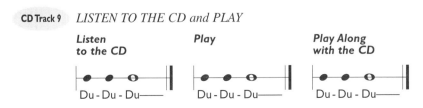

INSTRUMENT POSITION

Step 1: Position the trombone to the center of your body.

Step 2: Allow the downward angle of the trombone to be determined by your embouchure and mouthpiece placement.

Note: Be sure to support the entire weight of the trombone with your left hand and arm.

MARK ✔ or ? HERE

Step	1	2	3	4
	5	6	7	8
1				
2				

Step 3: Position your elbows comfortably away from your body.

3			

FOCUS ON TEACHING
Positive Reinforcement versus Negative Reinforcement

- A positive reinforcement uses words or actions to indicate approval of a student's response to a teacher initiative.

> Teacher initiative: "OK. Show me your instrument playing position."
> Positive reinforcement: "Ann, your instrument playing position is good, just like the photograph."

Suggestion: Use positive reinforcement to acknowledge both effort and achievement.

- A negative reinforcement uses words or actions to indicate disapproval of a student's response to a teacher initiative.

> Teacher initiative: "OK. Show me your instrument playing position."
> Negative reinforcement: "Tom, you're slouching."

Note: A negative reinforcement does not focus the student's attention on what to do.

Suggestion: Rather than give a negative reinforcement, show the student what you want them to do.

LEFT HAND POSITION

Step 1: Lock the slide.

Step 2: Form a "gun" with your first finger and thumb.

Step 3: Hook your thumb onto the lower cross brace of the bell section.

Step 4: Place your first finger on top of the mouthpiece shank.

Step 5: Wrap your remaining fingers around the inner slide cross brace.

Note: Keep your wrist straight.

	MARK ✔ or ? HERE			
Step	Week			
	1	2	3	4
	5	6	7	8
1				
2				
3				
4				
5				

RIGHT HAND POSITION

Step 1: Grasp the hand slide cross brace between the tip of your thumb and the tips of your first and second fingers.

Step 2: Curl your third and fourth fingers into your palm.

Note: Keep your wrist straight.

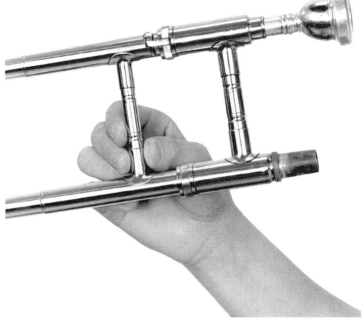

MARK ✔ or ? HERE

Step	Week			
	1	2	3	4
	5	6	7	8
1				
2				

FOCUS ON TEACHING

Assessment Informs and Motivates

- Assessment Provides Students with Vital Feedback
  - Assessment is a means to recognize and reward achievement
  - Assessment establishes need for practice
  - Assessment determines specific objectives for practice

Suggestion: Use checklists to recognize and record achievement. Employ teacher assessment, self-assessment, peer assessment, and adult home helper assessment.

LEARNING TO PRODUCE A TONE ON THE TROMBONE

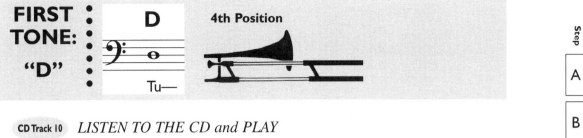

Step	MARK ✔ or ? HERE Week			
	1	2	3	4
	5	6	7	8
A				
B				
C				
D				

CD Track 10   *LISTEN TO THE CD and PLAY*

Listen to the CD   **Play**   **Play Along with the CD**

CD Track 11   *Call and Response – First Tone*

A. The embouchure is well formed.
B. The tone is started with the syllable "tu."
C. Tone quality and pitch resemble the model.
D. Posture is acceptable.
E. The right hand is well positioned.
F. The left hand is well positioned.

E			

F			

FOCUS ON TEACHING MUSIC PERFORMANCE
Telling Isn't Teaching

• To teach music performance is to show.

"I will show you what I want you to learn."

Suggestion: Use live demonstrations, visual media, and recordings to show students what is to be learned.

Asking Isn't Assessing

• To have learned to perform is to be able to show.

"Show me what you have learned."

Suggestion: Use student performances to assess music playing skills and music reading.

18

LEARNING TO PRODUCE ANOTHER TONE ON THE TROMBONE

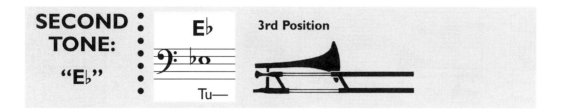

SECOND TONE: "E♭" E♭ 3rd Position Tu—

MARK ✔ or ? HERE				
Week				
Step	1	2	3	4
	5	6	7	8
A				
B				
C				
D				

CD Track 12 *LISTEN TO THE CD and PLAY*

Listen to the CD | Play | Play Along with the CD

Tu— | Tu—

CD Track 13 *Call and Response – First and Second Tones*

1 Listen Play 2 Listen Play 3 Listen Play 4 Listen Play

5 Listen Play 6 Listen Play 7 Listen Play 8 Listen Play

A. The embouchure is well formed.
B. The tone is started with the syllable "tu."
C. Tone quality and pitch resemble the model.
D. Posture is acceptable.
E. The right hand is well positioned.
F. The left hand is well positioned.

E				
F				

FOCUS ON TEACHING
Nonverbal Instruction versus Verbal Instruction

- A nonverbal teacher initiative uses actions rather than words to produce an intended result.

  Example: The teacher engages students in a call and response to illustrate the difference between separated and connected styles of articulation.

  Note: Nonverbal teaching saves time.

  Note: Students prefer nonverbal teaching over verbal teaching.

- A verbal teacher initiative uses words rather than actions to produce an intended result.

  Example: The teacher describes the difference between separated and connected styles of articulation.

  Note: Verbal teaching in the absence of a nonverbal model is often ineffective.

  Notable Exception: The verbal analogy can often be an effective means to connect common experience with an important musical concept.

  Example: One player with faulty intonation in a group of thirty creates a similar amount of distortion that one cloudy pane of glass creates in a row of thirty otherwise clear panes.

LEARNING TO PRODUCE A THIRD TONE ON THE TROMBONE

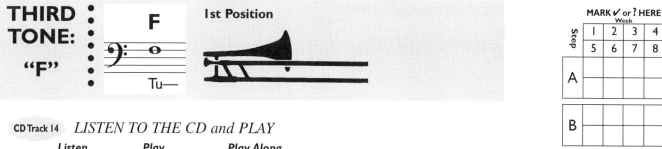

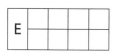

CD Track 14 *LISTEN TO THE CD and PLAY*

CD Track 15 *Call and Response – First, Second, and Third Tones*

A. The embouchure is well formed.
B. The tone is started with the syllable "tu."
C. Tone quality and pitch resemble the model.
D. Posture is acceptable.
E. The right hand is well positioned.
F. The left hand is well positioned.

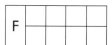

FOCUS ON TEACHING

One-to-One in Groups of Beginning Students

- Individual Lessons to Students in a Group Is an Inefficient Use of Time.

- Individual Lessons to Students in a Group Is a Highly Problematic Teaching Strategy.
  - Non-participating students often become inattentive and bored.
  - Bored students often become disruptive.
  - Disruptive student behavior often leads to negative and oppressive teacher behavior.

Suggestion: Attend to the needs of an individual student by engaging in peer group teaching and peer group assessment to maintain group focus.

Example: "Who can demonstrate an acceptable right hand position? ....OK!
Now, everyone take turns checking your stand partner's right hand position."

- Recorded Call and Response Tracks Provide a Means for the Teacher to Teach One-to-One.
  - The call and response is a highly effective and efficient group music learning strategy.
  - While all students are engaged in the call and response, the teacher is free to move about the class and attend to individual students who need instruction.

Suggestion: Use CD call and response tracks at the start of class to warm-up and to assess students one-to-one.

FIRST TUNE

Preparation to Play *Practice Every Day March*

CD Track 16   *Listen and Play*

Practice Every Day March

CD Track 1   **1.** *Listen*   **2.** *Listen and Play Along*   **CD Track 1-1**   *Play*

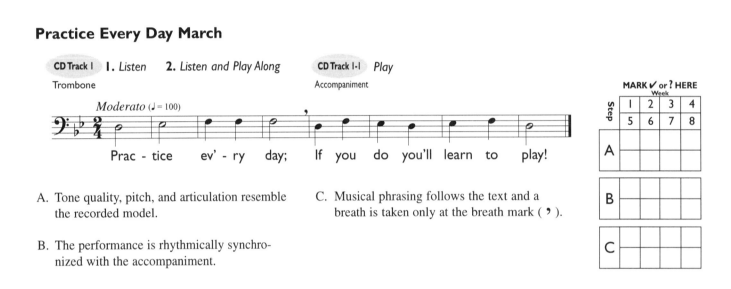

A. Tone quality, pitch, and articulation resemble the recorded model.

B. The performance is rhythmically synchronized with the accompaniment.

C. Musical phrasing follows the text and a breath is taken only at the breath mark (').

Step	Week			
	1	2	3	4
	5	6	7	8
A				
B				
C				

MARK ✔ or ? HERE

FOCUS ON TEACHING

Teach Patterns

• Music is composed of patterns.

• Patterns give meaning to music.

Note: Individual notes are to music what individual letters are to language - neither conveys much until they are grouped into meaningful patterns.

• Melodic patterns are the building blocks of musical phrases and musical form.

• Finger patterns are the building blocks of instrumental music performance.

Suggestion: Use teacher modeled or recorded call and response sequences to build pattern technique.

Suggestion: Employ rhythmic pattern flashcards and melodic pattern flashcards to teach pattern reading skills. *Band Home Helper* and *Do It! Play in Band.* www.giamusic.com

COMPOSITE ACHIEVEMENT CHECKLIST

✔ **If Satisfactory**   ❓ **If More Work Is Needed**

A. Posture

B. Instrument Position

C. Left Hand Position

D. Right Hand Position

E. Embouchure

F. Musical Phrasing

G. Musical Articulation

H. Tone Quality

MARK ✔ or ❓ HERE

Step	Week 1	2	3	4
	5	6	7	8
A				
B				
C				
D				
E				
F				
G				
H				

FOCUS ON TEACHING

The Keys to Effective Student Home Practice: Predicting, Discriminating, and Self-Remediation

- It is the teacher's responsibility to teach students to:

Predict, visually and aurally, specific objectives for practice.

"It Looks Like" - "It Sounds Like"

Discriminate the differences between visual and aural practice objectives and existing performance discrepancies.

"It Looks Like This" - "It Doesn't Look Like This"
"It Sounds Like This" - "It Doesn't Sound Like This"

Suggestion: Model both the performance objective and the performance discrepancy to teach students to discriminate the difference between "*What it is*" and "*What it isn't*."

Remediate performance problems with effective practice strategies.

"Use a mirror to look and compare."
"Use your CD player to listen and compare."
"Record performances to listen and compare."

Note: Effective home practice requires the same skills teachers need to teach well: the skills to predict, discriminate, and remediate.

FOCUS ON TEACHING

Assessment

Assessment of Music Achievement Requires Three Components:
- Specific, Observable Criteria
- An Aural or Visual Model for Reference
- A Record of Achievement

Assessment Takes Three Fundamental Forms:
- Teacher Assessment
- Peer Assessment
- Self-Assessment

Performance Achievement Checklist

1. PHYSICAL/TECHNICAL CRITERIA	EXEMPLARY	ACCEPTABLE	QUESTIONABLE	UNACCEPTABLE
A. Posture	☐	☐	☐	☐
B. Instrument Position	☐	☐	☐	☐
C. Left Hand Position	☐	☐	☐	☐
D. Right Hand Position	☐	☐	☐	☐
E. Embouchure	☐	☐	☐	☐
F. Breathing and Breath Control	☐	☐	☐	☐

2. MUSICAL CRITERIA	EXEMPLARY	ACCEPTABLE	QUESTIONABLE	UNACCEPTABLE
A. Tone Quality	☐	☐	☐	☐
B. Intonation	☐	☐	☐	☐
C. Articulation (Separated)	☐	☐	☐	☐
D. Articulation (Connected)	☐	☐	☐	☐
E. Musical Phrasing	☐	☐	☐	☐
F. Expressive Nuance	☐	☐	☐	☐

Suggestion: Use this "Permission to Copy" form to engage in Teacher Assessment, Peer Assessment, and Self-Assessment.

FOCUS ON TEACHING
"Sound" Teaching – The Achievement Loop

1. A "SOUND" MUSIC LEARNING OBJECTIVE

   The achievement loop starts with recorded music repertoire that is contained on the CD, performed by an artist, and set in an authentic music context that defines:

   - Tempo
   - Rhythm
   - Pitch
   - Melody
   - Phrasing
   - Tone Quality
   - Harmony
   - Expressive Nuance
   - Form

   A "sound" concept of the music learning objective motivates students for:

2. PREPARATION
   The teacher prepares the students for:

3. PRACTICE
   Practice leads to:

4. ACHIEVEMENT
   Student achievement pleases everyone and motivates the student to pursue:

5. A NEW "SOUND" MUSIC LEARNING OBJECTIVE
   A new achievement loop (1. above) starts with recorded music repertoire contained on the CD, performed by an artist, and set in an authentic music context.

FOCUS ON TEACHING
The Conditions for Learning[1]

In any classroom, the following conditions are necessary for efficient learning:

1. clearly delineated learning tasks
2. a stable environment
3. opportunity for self-selection of tasks
4. opportunity for independent work
5. closure and feedback (on achievement and behavior)

---

[1] Judith M. Smith and Donald E. P. Smith, *Classroom Management* (New York, N.Y.: Learning Research Associates, Inc., 1980).

FOCUS ON TEACHING

Singing – A Primary Tool for Teaching and Assessing

- Singing Develops Important Musical Skills.
- Singing Develops Concepts that Guide Home Practice.
- Singing Provides a Means to Assess Fundamental Musicianship.

   Note: Students sing about as well as they hear.

Suggestion 1: Always sing to recorded models or accompaniments.

Suggestion 2: Accompany singing with rhythmic movement such as a lap-pat or heel-tap.

BALLAD – *A short, simple song in a narrative or descriptive style*

Model Tr. 17
Accom. Tr. 17-1

❶ Cowboy Ballad

Legato

Cow - boy, cow - boy, rid - ing West. Clip - clop, clip - clop, need to rest.
Git - up, git - on move a - long. Hear me sing my sad old song.

Model Tr. 18
Accom. Tr. 18-1

❷ Stepping and Skipping

Moderato

Step - ping, step - ping, step - ping up. Skip - ping, skip - ping, step and skip.

Model Tr. 19
Accom. Tr. 19-1

❸ Notes

Moderato

Notes step down, notes step up. Notes re - peat and notes can skip.

FOCUS ON TEACHING

Rhythmic Movement - A Primary Tool for Teaching and Assessing

- Rhythm is the organizing principle of music performance.

   - Rhythm is what makes music move.
   - Rhythm is what holds music together.

- The ability to synchronize rhythmic movement to music is an important prerequisite to the development of music listening, reading, writing, and performance skills. Moving well to music is also an aesthetic experience.

   - We learn rhythm best by listening and moving.

Suggestion: Use synchronous rhythmic movement to music to demonstrate steady beat for students.[1] Examples of synchronous rhythmic movement include heel-taps, lap-pats, toe-taps, finger-snaps, and hand-claps.

- Movement to music provides a means to assess rhythmic musicianship. One element of rhythmic musicianship is the ability to synchronize movement to the primary beat of music.

   - The primary beat of music is best defined by the ictus of the conductor's baton.

Suggestion: To assess students' understanding of the primary beat in music, direct them to close their eyes, listen to the music, and lap-pat the primary beat in time with the music.

[1] Refer to *Movement to Music in Confined Spaces* (Weikart and Froseth, MLR-188); *Music For Movement* (Blaser and Froseth, MLR 187CD); and *Move to the Sound of World Music* (Froseth, CD-668). www.giamusic.com

FOCUS ON TEACHING
Starting D – C – B♭ versus D – E♭ – F

- Some Students May Be More Successful Descending D – C – B♭
- Some Students May Be More Successful Ascending D – E♭ – F

Suggestion: Adjust the sequence of repertoire when appropriate and necessary to help students succeed.

FOLK SONG – *A song reflecting the traditions of the people of a country or region and forming part of their characteristic culture.*

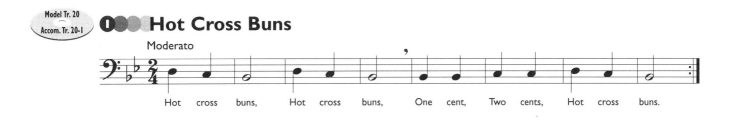

LULLABY – *A cradle song, usually sung by a mother to soothe or quiet an infant before bedtime.*

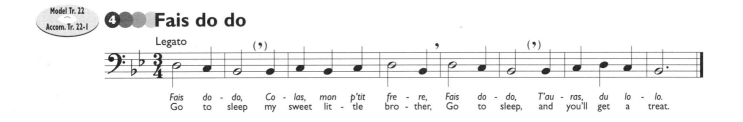

FOCUS ON TEACHING
Learning What Something "Is Not" Can Help Teach What Something "Is"

- Major Tonality Is Not Minor Tonality
- Minor Tonality Is Not Major Tonality

Suggestion: Use CD models to contrast the different sounds of major tonality and minor tonality.

TONALITY – A characteristic of Western music referring to the relationship of pitches to a specific tonal center. If Do is the tonal center, the tonality is Major. If La is the tonal center, the tonality is Minor.

Model Tr. 23
Accom. Tr. 23-1

1 Au Claire de la Lune (IN MINOR TONALITY)

French Folk Song

Model Tr. 24
Accom. Tr. 24-1

2 Fais do do (IN MINOR TONALITY)

French Lullaby

FOCUS ON TEACHING
Musical Independence

- Musical Rounds Help to Develop Musical Independence
- Musical Rounds Prepare Students for Ensemble Performance

Suggestion: Allow students to determine when to enter the round without help.

ROUND – A specially composed melody that allows two or more individuals to create interesting musical effects by starting the melody at different times.

3 Lady My (2-PART ROUND)

English Round

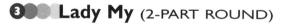
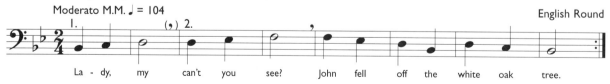

4 Be-A-Round (4-PART ROUND)

English Round

FOCUS ON TEACHING
The Power of Music Modeling

Recorded and Live Music Models Serve to:

- Define Performance Objectives
- Exemplify Performance Objectives
- Motivate Students to Practice and Play

Suggestion: Always listen first to the recorded artist model on your CD before you begin to practice. A well developed concept of the objective is essential to guide one to the desired outcome.

FOCUS ON TEACHING
Musical Context

Recorded Accompaniments Provide Musical Context that Informs Students about:

- Tempo
- Rhythm
- Intonation
- Melody
- Tone Quality
- Timbre
- Harmony
- Form
- Expressive Nuance
- Musical Style

Suggestion: Practice until you are able to play along with the model and accompaniment tracks on your CD.

28

Accom. Tr. 20-1

1 **Hot Cross Buns**

Moderato   English Folk Song

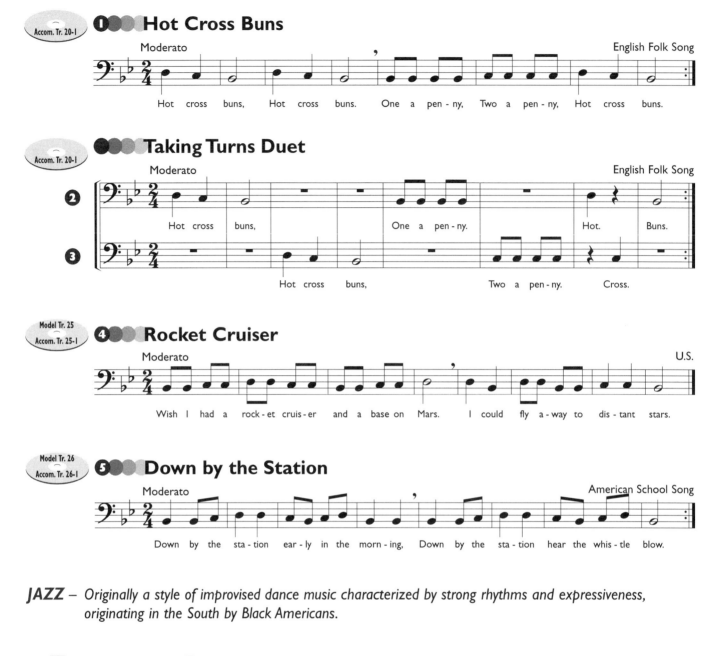

Hot cross buns,   Hot cross buns.   One a pen-ny,   Two a pen-ny,   Hot cross buns.

Accom. Tr. 20-1

Taking Turns Duet

Moderato   English Folk Song

2

Hot cross buns,   One a pen-ny.   Hot.   Buns.

3

Hot cross buns,   Two a pen-ny.   Cross.

Model Tr. 25
Accom. Tr. 25-1

4 **Rocket Cruiser**

Moderato   U.S.

Wish I had a rock-et cruis-er and a base on Mars.   I could fly a-way to dis-tant stars.

Model Tr. 26
Accom. Tr. 26-1

5 **Down by the Station**

Moderato   American School Song

Down by the sta-tion ear-ly in the morn-ing,   Down by the sta-tion hear the whis-tle blow.

JAZZ – *Originally a style of improvised dance music characterized by strong rhythms and expressiveness, originating in the South by Black Americans.*

Model Tr. 27
Accom. Tr. 28

6 **★SOLO★** **Down by the Station** (SWINGING JAZZ STYLE "BY EAR" STARTING ON B♭ – WITH REPEAT)

IMPROVISATION – *The art of creating music spontaneously, during performance. Also, a form of composition.*

RHYTHMIC IMPROVISATION – *The act of expressing one's own rhythmic ideas while maintaining the basic melodic character of the piece.*

Accom. Tr. 28

7 **★SOLO★** **Improvise Rhythmic Variations On** *Down By the Station*

Accom. Tr. 19-1

Eighth Notes Duet

Moderato   U.S.

8

9

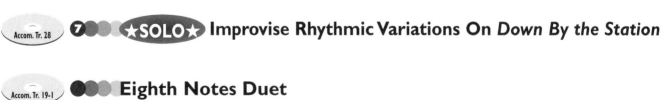

FOCUS ON TEACHING
Creating a Safe Environment for Spontaneous Music Making

 Down By the Station (JAZZ STYLE)

PRINCIPLE A: KEEP IT SIMPLE (Too many options can inhibit creativity)

    PROCEDURE 1: Direct students to "Use the tones Concert B♭, C, and D"

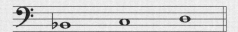

PRINCIPLE B: KEEP EVERYONE INVOLVED (Peer observation can be intimidating)

    PROCEDURE 2: Teach everyone an 8-beat riff (melodic ostinato)
    (NOTE: Riffs may be improvised and taught to the class by the teacher or by students)

Example (As notated)

Example (As performed in a swinging style ²₄ ♫ = ⁶₈ ♩. ♪)

    PROCEDURE 3: Direct students to "Repeat the riff until the music ends"

PRINCIPLE C: ALLOW FOR SELF-SELECTION OF TASKS *(A strategy designed to avoid the no–play freeze)*

    PROCEDURE 4: When individual students are chosen or volunteer, suggest that they:

    A. "Play the riff"

    B. "Improvise rhythmic variations on the riff, or"

    C. "Improvise rhythmic/melodic variations on the riff"

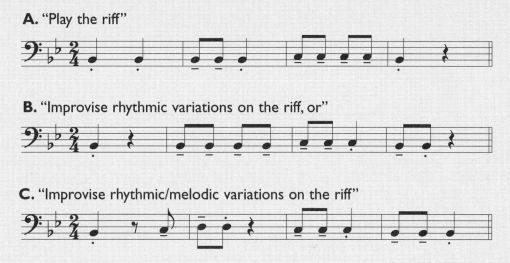

PRINCIPLE D: AVOID COMMON CREATIVITY KILLERS INCLUDING EXPRESSIONS OF APPROVAL OR DISAPPROVAL, SURVEILLANCE, EVALUATION, REWARD SYSTEMS, AND COMPETITION

FOCUS ON TEACHING

Summary of Strategies for Creating Music Improvisations That Are Interesting and Well-Structured

 Down By the Station (JAZZ STYLE)

REGGAE – A musical style mixing African and Caribbean rhythms often attributed to Jamaican sources.

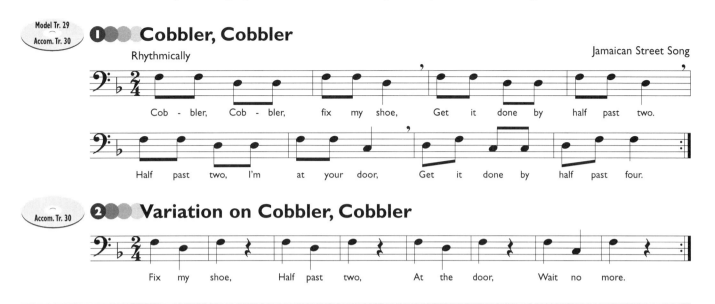

FOCUS ON TEACHING
Don't Slow It Down; Break It Down

Step 1. Analyze the Composition for Number of Melodic Patterns
Cobbler, Cobbler is composed of three different 4-beat melodic patterns

Step 2. Decompose Each Pattern and then Recompose Each in a Sequence that Progresses from Easier Patterns to the Composed Pattern

Step 3. Employ the Teacher Call/Student Response to Develop the Technique and Articulation Skills Required to Play *Cobbler, Cobbler*

Teacher: "The starting note of the first pattern is F"

Suggestion: Maintain the tempo of the CD model of *Cobbler, Cobbler*.

This symbol indicates that the Left Speaker to Right speaker balance of the music can be controlled by the Speaker Balance Control Knob on your stereo. For accompaniment only, turn the Speaker Balance Control Knob to the extreme right.

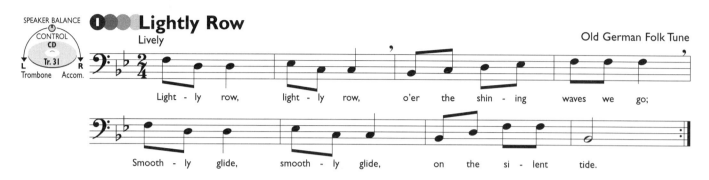

DIXIELAND JAZZ – *An early style of African American jazz music originating in new Orleans*

AURAL TRANSCRIPTION – *Learning to play recorded music "by ear" without the aid of music notation. Also, the transfer of music heard to notation.*

2 ★SOLO★ **Play *When the Saints Go Marching In* Starting On B♭**

FOCUS ON TEACHING
The Values of Learning to Play "By Ear"

• Playing "By Ear" Is an Important and Useful Musical Skill
• Playing "By Ear" Develops a Connection Between the Musical Ear and the Hand
• Playing "By Ear" Allows Students to Pursue Their Musical Interests Independently

BLUES – *An African American folk music characterized by spontaneity and deep emotions.*

CALL AND RESPONSE – *A musical alteration between two performers or a performer and a group of performers. The musical response to the call may be imitated or improvised.*

  **Blues in F** (IMITATED RESPONSE – "BY EAR" STARTING ON F)

  **Blues in F** (IMPROVISED RESPONSE – "BY EAR" STARTING ON ANY NOTE)

  **Improvise Over the 12-Bar Blues in F**

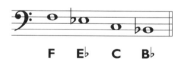

F   E♭   C   B♭

FOCUS ON TEACHING
The Components of a Performance-Based Listening Experience

• Listen - to focus attention on sound
• Hear - to comprehend with the ear
• Respond - to perform what is heard

Suggestion: Use aural transcription and call and response to assess how well students are listening and hearing.

THEME AND VARIATIONS – *A musical form based upon a melody followed by a succession of composed rhythmic/melodic variations.*

COUNTRY MUSIC – *A popular style of music that originated in the American South and West.*

SPECIAL PROJECT – Learn to Play a Song "By Ear"

❹ ★SOLO★ **Play *Jingle Bells* Starting on D**

❺ **Day Is Done** (4-PART ROUND)

34

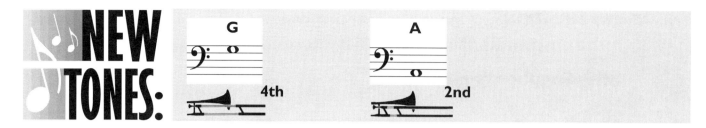

NEW TONES:

G	A
4th	2nd

D.C. AL FINE – *Go back to the beginning and end at the fine.*

SPEAKER BALANCE
CONTROL
CD
Tr. 39
L   R
Trombone   Accom.

❶ Twinkle, Twinkle, Little Star (SOLO, DUET, TRIO, OR QUARTET)

French Folk Tune
Text by Jane and Ann Taylor (1806)

Smoothly

Twin - kle, twin - kle, lit - tle star, How I won - der what you are.

D.C. al fine

Up a - bove the world so high, like a dia - mond in the sky.

❷ Harmony Part One to *Twinkle, Twinkle, Little Star*

Softly and smoothly

❸ Harmony Part Two to *Twinkle, Twinkle, Little Star*

Softly and smoothly

❹ ☆ Obbligato to *Twinkle, Twinkle, Little Star*

Softly and smoothly

SWING STYLE – *A type of Big Band jazz of the late 1930s and 1940s.*

Model Tr. 40
Accom. Tr. 41

❺ ★SOLO★ Twinkle, Twinkle, Little Star (SWING STYLE "BY EAR" STARTING ON B♭)

Model Tr. 42
Accom. Tr. 42-1

① Die Abendglocke (Evening Bells)
Oh, How Lovely Is the Evening (3–PART ROUND)

German Round

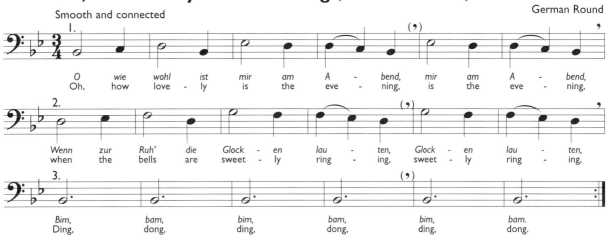

Smooth and connected

1.
O wie wohl ist mir am A - bend, mir am A - bend,
Oh, how love - ly is the eve - ning, is the eve - ning,

2.
Wenn zur Ruh' die Glock - en lau - ten, Glock - en lau - ten,
when the bells are sweet - ly ring - ing, sweet - ly ring - ing,

3.
Bim, bam, bim, bam, bim, bam.
Ding, dong, ding, dong, ding, dong.

SPEAKER BALANCE
CONTROL
CD
Tr. 43
L R
Vibra-phone Accom.

② Cuckoo Song

Germany

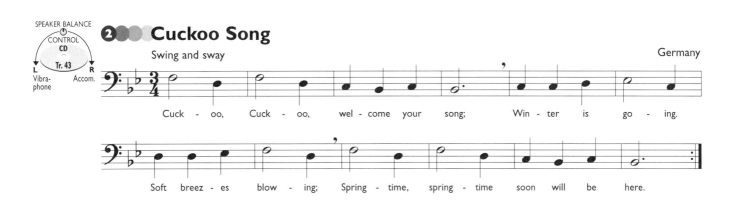

Swing and sway

Cuck - oo, Cuck - oo, wel - come your song; Win - ter is go - ing.

Soft breez - es blow - ing; Spring - time, spring - time soon will be here.

SPECIAL PROJECT – Learn to Play a Song "By Ear"

③ ★SOLO★ Play *Fais do do* Starting on G

④ Round Evening (4–PART ROUND)

U.S.

Smoothly M.M. ♩ = 56

⑤ Round Evening Two (4–PART ROUND)

U.S.

Smoothly M.M. ♩ = 56

Round Evening and *Round Evening Two* may be played simultaneously.

Model Tr. 44
Accom. Tr. 44-1

❶◼◼◼ **By the Fireside** (SOLO, DUET, TRIO, OR QUARTET)

U.S.

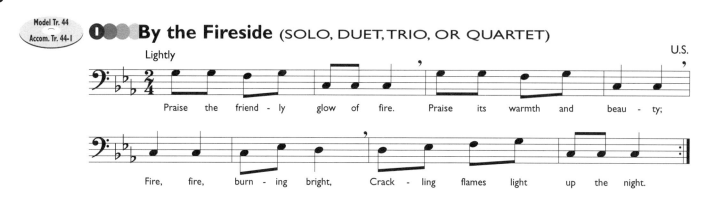

Lightly

Praise the friend - ly glow of fire. Praise its warmth and beau - ty;

Fire, fire, burn - ing bright, Crack - ling flames light up the night.

Model Tr. 44

❷◼◼◼ **Accompaniment One to *By the Fireside***

Softly

Model Tr. 44

❸◼◼◼ **Accompaniment Two to *By the Fireside***

Softly and lightly

Model Tr. 44

❹☆◼ **Obbligato to *By the Fireside***

Softly and lightly

❺◼◼◼ **Round Dance** (4–PART ROUND IN MINOR TONALITY)

U.S.

Lightly M.M. ♩ = 132

1.   2.   3.   4.

❻◼◼◼ **S'evivon Round (Spin, My Top)** (2–PART ROUND)

Hebrew Song

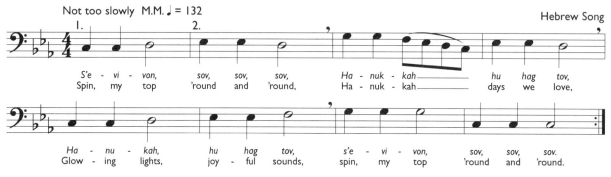

Not too slowly M.M. ♩ = 132

1.   2.

S'e - vi - von, sov, sov, sov, Ha - nuk - kah_____ hu hag tov,
Spin, my top 'round and 'round, Ha - nuk - kah_____ days we love,

Ha - nu - kah, hu hag tov, s'e - vi - von, sov, sov, sov.
Glow - ing lights, joy - ful sounds, spin, my top 'round and 'round.

REMINDER: "A"

2nd

HYMN – A song of worship.

Model Tr. 45
Accom. Tr. 45-1

Vesper Hymn (SOLO OR DUET)

Russian Folk Tune
Text by Thomas Moore

Smooth and connected

1a / 2a: Hark! The Ves - per Hymn is steal - ing o'er the wa - ters soft and clear;

1b / 2b: Near - er yet and near - er peal - ing. Soft it breaks up - on the ear.

We Are Met (4-PART ROUND)

Brightly M.M. ♩ = 120

Samuel Webbe (c. 1680)

We are met let mirth a - bound, and let the catch and glee go 'round.

French Cathedrals (3-PART ROUND)

Stately M.M. ♩ = 94

French Lullaby

Or - lé - ans, Beau - gen - cy, No - tre Dame— de Clé - ry, Ven - dô - me, Ven - dô - me.

Accom. Tr. 30

SPECIAL PROJECT – **Return to *Cobbler, Cobbler* on Page 31 to Improvise**

★SOLO★ **Use the tones F, G, D, C, and A**

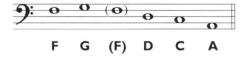

F   G   (F)   D   C   A

FOCUS ON TEACHING

Creating a Safe Environment for Spontaneous Music Making

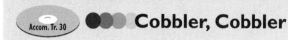 **Cobbler, Cobbler**

PRINCIPLE A: KEEP IT SIMPLE (Too many options can inhibit creativity)

PROCEDURE 1: Direct students to "Use the tones F, D, and C"

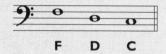

PRINCIPLE B: KEEP EVERYONE INVOLVED (Peer observation can be intimidating)

PROCEDURE 2: Teach everyone an 8-beat riff (melodic ostinato)
(NOTE: Riffs may be improvised and taught to the class by the teacher or by students)

PROCEDURE 3: Direct students to "Repeat the riff until the music ends"

PRINCIPLE C: ALLOW FOR SELF-SELECTION OF TASKS *(Absence of options can stifle creativity)*

PROCEDURE 4: When individual students are chosen or volunteer, suggest that they:

A. "Play the riff"

B. "Improvise rhythmic variations on the riff"

C. "Improvise melodic/rhythmic variations on the riff"

PRINCIPLE D: AVOID COMMON CREATIVITY KILLERS INCLUDING EXPRESSIONS OF APPROVAL OR DISAPPROVAL, SURVEILLANCE, EVALUATION, REWARD SYSTEMS, AND COMPETITION

FOCUS ON TEACHING
Developing and Assessing Musical Independence

- Multi-Level Musical Rounds Offer Expanded Opportunities for Developing and Assessing Musical Independence
- *Little Bells of Westminster* Makes Provision for 12 Students to Perform Independent Entrances (4 + 4 + 4) at 3 Levels of Difficulty (Lines 1, 2, 3).

Suggestion: Allow students to determine when to enter the round without help.

❶ Little Bells of Westminster (4-PART ROUND)

❷ Variation One on Little Bells of Westminster (4-PART ROUND)

❸ Variation Two on Little Bells of Westminster (4-PART ROUND)

Little Bells of Westminster, Variation One, and Variation Two may be played simultaneously.

❹ Two Birds (4-PART ROUND)

❺ Rooster Round (5-PART ROUND)

40

Model Tr. 46
Accom. Tr. 47

1 **Little Tom Tinker** (4-PART ROUND)

Lively   Traditional Round

1.   2.

Lit - tle Tom Tin - ker got burned by a clink - er and he be - gan to cry.

3.   4.

"Ma!"_____   "Ma!"_____   Poor lit - tle in - no - cent guy.

Accom. Tr. 47

2 **Variation on** *Little Tom Tinker*

1.   2.   3.   4.

Tom - my Tin - ker cried and cried. "Ma!"____ "Ma!"____ my, oh, my.

Model Tr. 48
Accom. Tr. 48-1

3 **Oats, Peas, Beans**

Lively   England

Oats, peas, beans, and bar - ley grow, Oats, peas, beans, and bar - ley grow; Can

you or I or an - y - one know how Oats, peas, beans, and bar - ley grow?

Accom. Tr. 48-1

4 **Variation on** *Oats, Peas, Beans*

Model Tr. 49
Accom. Tr. 49-1

5 **Patsy Ory-Ory-Aye**

Lively   Irish Railroad Song

1. Eigh - teen hund - red nine - ty - one, That's the year that I be - gun,
2. Pat - sy O - ry - O - ry - Aye, Pat - sy O - ry - O - ry - Aye,

That's the year that I be - gun, A - work - ing on the rail - road.
Pat - sy O - ry - O - ry - Aye, A - work - ing on the rail - road.

FOCUS ON TEACHING
Success Is a Powerful Motivator

• Students need to have at least one acknowledged performance success during the course of every class.
• An easy variation can allow students to have a successful experience.
• An easy variation can give students motivation to practice for success with more challenging material.

Suggestion: Develop teaching strategies that orchestrate success in your classroom.

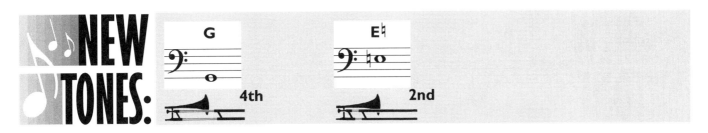

SPEAKER BALANCE
CONTROL
CD
Tr. 50
L   R
Trombone   Accom.

① Hatikvah

With expression

Hebrew Melody

Play along
Tr. 51

② SPECIAL PROJECT – Let's Go Blue! – Play Along

★SOLO★ "By Ear" Use the tones B♭, D, E♭, E♮, and F

B♭   D   E♭   E♮   F

③ SPECIAL PROJECT

★SOLO★ *Hot Cross Buns* "By Ear" Starting on A

English Folk Song

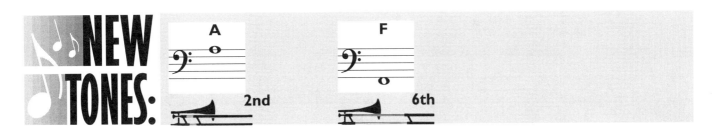

Accom. Tr. 35

Tracking the Blues in F (Concert)

In a swinging style

42

NEW TONE: Ab 3rd

SPEAKER BALANCE
CONTROL
CD
Tr. 52
L R
Trombone Accom.

❶ Bingo

American Folk Song

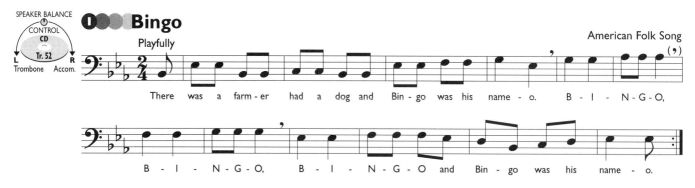

Playfully

There was a farm-er had a dog and Bin-go was his name-o. B - I - N - G - O,

B - I - N - G - O, B - I - N - G - O and Bin-go was his name-o.

BALLAD – *A short, simple song in a narrative or descriptive form, sometimes set to a romantic or historical poem.*

Model Tr. 53
Accom. Tr. 53-1

❷ Aura Lee

American Ballad

Gently

As the black-bird in the spring, 'Neath the wil-low tree,_____

Sat and piped, I heard him sing, Sing - ing Au - ra Lee.

Au - ra Lee, Au - ra Lee, Maid of gold - en hair,

Sun - shine came a - long with thee, And swal - lows in the air.

BLUES ROCK – *A musical style that merges blues harmonies with rock and roll rhythms of the 1950s and 1960s.*

Call and Response
Tr. 54

❸ SPECIAL PROJECT – **Blues Rock "Call and Response"**

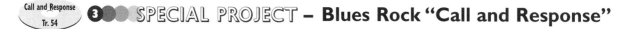

⭐SOLO⭐ **Blues Rock** (IMITATED RESPONSE) **Use the tones F, D, G, and Ab**

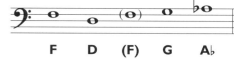

F   D   (F)   G   Ab

⭐SOLO⭐ **Blues Rock** (IMPROVISED RESPONSE) **Use the tones Bb, D, F, G, and Ab**

Bb   D   F   G   Ab

BOUFFONS – *Costumed dancers of the 15th and 16th centuries.*

Model Tr. 55
Accom. Tr. 55-1

Bouffons (SOLO OR DUET)

Thoinot Arbeau (ca. 1519–1595)

Briskly

SPEAKER BALANCE
CONTROL
CD
Tr. 56
L   R
Trombone   Accom.

Now the Day Is Over

Sir Joseph Barnby (1838–1896)

Smoothly M.M. ♩ = 92

Now the day is o - ver; Night is draw - ing nigh.

Shad - ows of the eve - ning, Steal a - cross the sky.

Model Tr. 57
Accom. Tr. 57-1

The Birch Tree (THEME FROM THE FOURTH SYMPHONY)

Russian Folk song
Tschaikovsky (1840–1893)

Tenuto

44

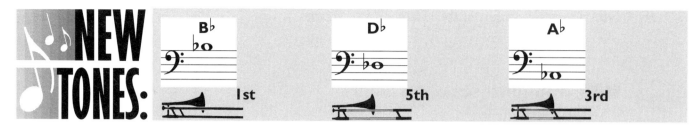

FOLK HYMN – A song of worship with a religious text that has been set to a folk melody.

❶ Amazing Grace

John Newell (1779)
Early American Melody

A - maz - ing— grace how sweet the sound that saved a — wretch like— me!_____ I

❷ Amazing Grace Harmony Part One

once— was— lost but now I'm— found; Was blind but— now I see._____

❸ Amazing Grace Harmony Part (BASS LINE)

GOSPEL – African-American church music characterized by expression, improvisation, and a strong sense of celebration.

Model Tr. 58
Accom. Tr. 58-1

❹ ★SOLO★ Amazing Grace (GOSPEL STYLE – "BY EAR" STARTING ON B♭)

Accom. Tr. 58-1

❺ ★SOLO★ Amazing Grace (IMPROVISE IN GOSPEL STYLE – "BY EAR" STARTING ON B♭)

❻ Tallis Canon (4-PART CANON)

Legato M.M. ♩ = 96

Thomas Tallis (1510–1585)

All praise to Thee, my Lord, this night. For all the bles - sings of the

light; keep me, Oh keep us, King of Kings, Be - neath Thine own Al - might - y wings.

NEW TONE: C — 3rd

Model Tr. 59 / Accom. Tr. 60

1. Scarborough Fair (DORIAN MODE)

Smoothly with expression — English Ballad

Are you going to Scar-bo-rough Fair? Pars-ley, sage, rose-mar-y, and thyme. Oh, send my love to one who lives there, Once she was a true love of mine.

2. The Hart, He Loves the High Wood (4-PART ROUND)

With humor and enthusiasm M.M. ♩ = 132 — Composer Unknown ca. 1680

The hart, he loves the high wood, The hare, he loves the hill. The knight, he loves a bright sword, The la-dy loves her will.

3. Row, Row, Row Your Boat (4-PART ROUND)

Merrily M.M. ♩. = 104 — U.S. E. O. Lyte

Row, row, row your boat gent-ly down the stream. Mer-ri-ly mer-ri-ly mer-ri-ly mer-ri-ly Life is but a dream.

4. Time and Tide (2-PART ROUND)

Marcato M.M. ♩ = 100–108 — Lowell Mason (1864)

Time and tide will wait for no-one.

5. Shave and a Haircut

As quickly as possible — Early American

Shave and a hair-cut, TWO BITS!

SPEAKER BALANCE
CONTROL
CD
Tr. 61
L   R
Tuba   Accom.

Sur le Pont d'Avignon (On the Bridge of Avignon) Duet

Lively   French Folk Song

Sur   le   pont,   d'A - vi - gnon   L'on - y   dan - se,   L'on - y   dan - se.
On   the   bridge,   A - vi - gnon   Eve - ry - one   is   dan - cing,   dan - cing.

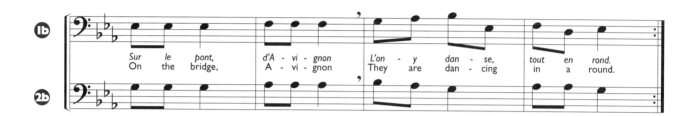

Sur   le   pont,   d'A - vi - gnon   L'on - y   dan - se,   tout   en   rond.
On   the   bridge,   A - vi - gnon   They   are   dan - cing   in   a   round.

Melodic Ostinatos to Sur le Pont d'Avignon

Singing Goose (4-PART ROUND)

Moderato M.M. ♩ = 100   England

Why   should - n't   my   goose,   Sing   as   well   as   thy   goose,

When   I   paid   for   my   goose,   Twice   as   much   as   thou?

Santy Maloney (4-PART ROUND)

Spirited M.M. ♩ = 100   England

Can   you   dance   San - ty   Ma - lon - ey?   Can   you   dance   San - ty   Ma - lon - ey?

Can   you   dance   San - ty   Ma - lon - ey,   As   we   go   round   a - bout?

HIGH LIFE – *A popular song and dance style of West Africa (Ghana) that blends African and Western instruments and musical characteristics; it can occur in duple or triple meter and features rhythmic and melodic ostinati.*

48

SAMBA – A Brazilian dance music form in duple meter.

Down A'Round and Up Again #1, #2, and #3 may be played simultaneously.

PARTNER SONGS* – *Songs that may be played simultaneously to a common accompaniment.*

*A-Workin' on the Railroad; Oats, Peas, Beans; Bluebird; and The Mulberry Bush are Partner Songs

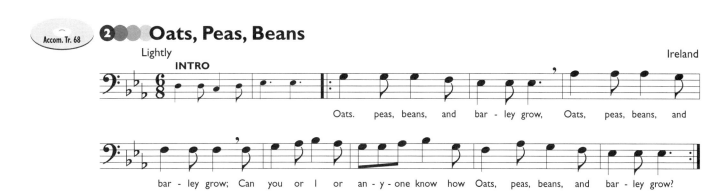

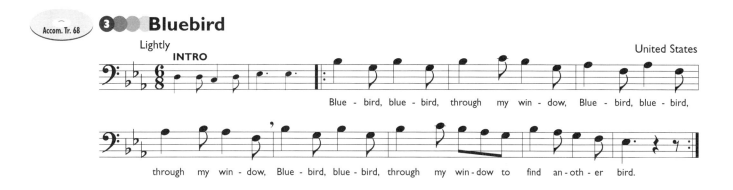

50

① Barbara Allen

Plaintively

Scotland

In Scar - let town where I was born, There was a fair maid dwell - in', Made

ev - 'ry youth cry—— "well - a - way," Her name was Bar - bara Al - len. In Al - len.

② Music Alone Shall Live (3-PART ROUND)

Spirited M.M. ♩ = 116

Traditional

Mu - sic a - lone shall live nev - er to die. Mu - sic a - lone shall live,

Mu - sic a - lone shall live, Mu - sic a - lone shall live nev - er to die.

③ Melodic Ostinatos to *Music Alone Shall Live*

ⓐ

ⓑ

ⓒ

ⓓ

④ Lullaby Round (9-PART ROUND)

Smoothly

Traditional

Lul - la - lul - la - by, lul - la - by, lul - la - by sweet - ly sing to lul - la -

by, lul - la - by, lul - la - by, sweet - ly sing to lul - la - by.

⑤ SPECIAL PROJECT – Return to *Cobbler, Cobbler* on Page 31 to Improvise

FOCUS ON TEACHING

A Special Individualized Option for Spontaneous Music Making

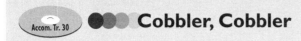 **Cobbler, Cobbler**

MUSICAL PARAPHRASE – An improvised conversation between two performers. The conversation begins with a 4-beat improvised "Call." The "Response" is a 4-beat restatement (paraphrase) of the "Call" using a slightly different combination of tones, rhythm, and/or articulations.

Direct students to employ one of the following options:

A. "Use the tones F, D, and C" or   **B.** "Use the tones G, F, D, and C"

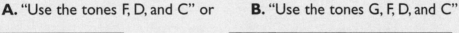

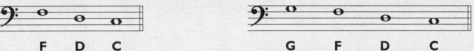

EXAMPLE OF OPTION A:

"The starting note is F"

Suggestion: To reduce student apprehension, involve students in group paraphrased responses.

EXAMPLE OF OPTION B:

"The starting note is F"

Suggestion: Always ask for volunteers when engaging in individual student paraphrased responses.

Another Option for Spontaneous Music Making

• Ask volunteers to lead the class with their own improvised calls (vocal or instrumental).

• Direct the class to follow with imitated or improvised responses.

52

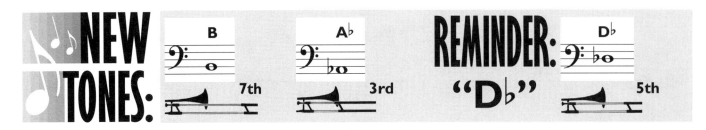

Greensleeves

England

Smoothly with expression

A - las my love— you do me wrong,. To cast me off dis - court - eous - ly. And I have loved— you

for so long,_ De - light - ing in— your com - pan - y. Green - sleeves. was all my joy,— Green - sleeves was

my de - light, Green - sleeves was my heart of gold,— And who but my la - dy Green - sleeves.

Lullaby Round (9-PART SCALE ROUND)

Traditional

Smoothly

Lul - la - lul - la - by, lul - la - by, lul - la - by sweet - ly sing to lul - la -

by, lul - la - by, lul - la - by, sweet - ly sing to lul - la - by.

Rise Up, O Flame (4-PART ROUND)

England

Stately M.M. ♩. = 46, ♪ = 138

Blow the Winds Southerly (4-PART SCALE ROUND)

Old Sea Chanty

Swing and sway M.M. ♩. = 46, ♪ = 138

Blow the winds south - er - ly, south - er - ly, south - er - ly, Blow the winds o - ver the sea.

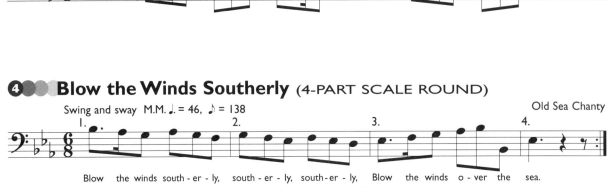

Simple Gifts

Lyrically
INTRO

Shaker Tune

'Tis the gift to be sim-ple, 'Tis the gift to be free, 'Tis the gift to come down where we ought to be, And when we find our-selves— in the place just— right, it will be in the val-ley of Love and De-light. When true sim-pli-ci-ty is gained, to bow and to bend we will not be a-shamed. To turn— and to turn— will— be our de-light, 'til by turn-ing, turn-ing we come 'round right.

Saint Paul's Steeple (SCALE SONG AND DUET)

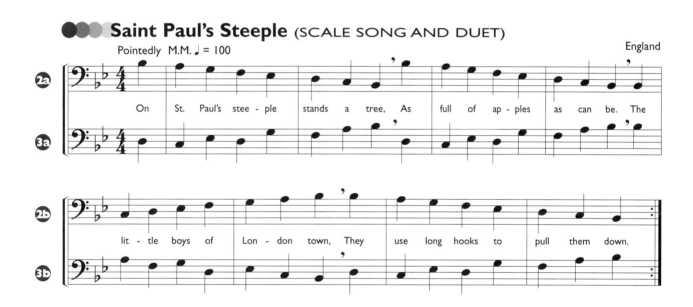

Pointedly M.M. ♩ = 100

England

On St. Paul's stee-ple stands a tree, As full of ap-ples as can be. The lit-tle boys of Lon-don town, They use long hooks to pull them down.

Chumbara (SCALE SONG)

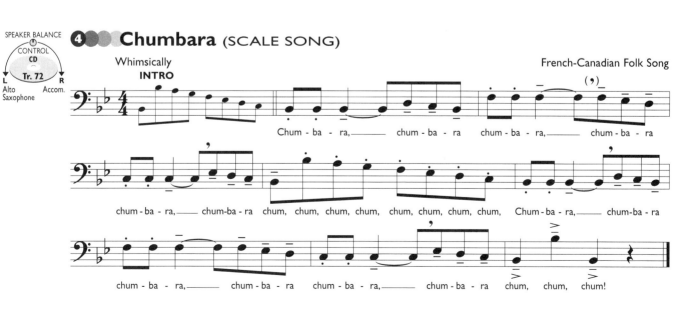

Whimsically
INTRO

French-Canadian Folk Song

Chum-ba-ra,— chum-ba-ra chum-ba-ra,— chum-ba-ra chum-ba-ra,— chum-ba-ra chum, chum, chum, chum, chum, chum, chum, chum, Chum-ba-ra,— chum-ba-ra chum-ba-ra,— chum-ba-ra chum-ba-ra,— chum-ba-ra chum, chum, chum!

54

SEIS – *A traditional song of dance music style of Puerto Rico in duple meter.*

❶ Habemos Llegado (PLAY ALONG)

Lightly

Puerto Rican Folk Song

Ha - be - mos lle - ga - do a su a -
We're here with our song, all you

ma - do ho - gar.
peo - ple to greet.
Ha - be - mos lle - ga - do a su a - ma - do ho - gar,
We're here with our song, all you peo - ple to greet,

1a
con con - chas, con per - las, con bri - sas del mar; con
with conch shells and pearls and sea breez - es so sweet; with

2a

1b
con - chas, con per - las, con bri - sas del mar.
conch shells and pearls and sea breez - es so sweet.

2b

❸ Aeolian Scale (NATURAL MINOR SCALE)

M.M. ♩ = 88

❹ Old Abram Brown (NATURAL MINOR SCALE ROUND)

Heavy and sad M.M. ♩ = 88

Traditional

Old A - bram Brown is dead and gone we'll ne - ver see him more. He

used to wear an old grey coat, all but - toned down be - fore. Old fore.

SYNCOPATION – *A displacement of the natural pulse or accent of the music, usually to the second half of the beat, as in:* ♪ ♩. *and* ♪ ♩ ♪

SPECIAL PROJECT – "Call and Response"

❶ ●●●● ★SOLO★ **Learn to Look, Listen, and Replicate What You See and Hear**

Do As I Do

SPEAKER BALANCE
CONTROL
CD
Tr. 75
L — R
Trombone   Accom.

❷ ●●● **John Henry**

United States

Robustly
INTRO

 NEW TONE:

F#
𝄢 ♯𝅗𝅥
5th

SPEAKER BALANCE
CONTROL
CD
Tr. 76
L — R
Cornet   Accom.

❸ ●●● **Saint James Infirmary**

United States

In a swinging style ♪♪ = ♪♪

❹ ●●● **Canoe Round** (4-PART ROUND)

United States

With enthusiasm

My pad - dle's keen and bright, flash-ing with sil - ver. Fol - low the wild goose flight, dip, dip, and swing.

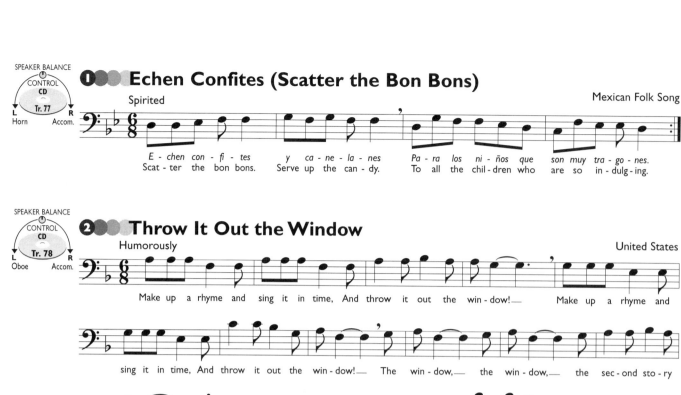

❶ Echen Confites (Scatter the Bon Bons)

Spirited

Mexican Folk Song

SPEAKER BALANCE
CONTROL
CD
Tr. 77
Horn   Accom.

E - chen con - fi - tes   y   ca - ne - la - nes   Pa - ra   los   ni - ños   que   son   muy   tra - go - nes.
Scat - ter   the   bon bons.   Serve   up   the   can - dy.   To   all   the   chil - dren   who   are   so   in - dulg - ing.

❷ Throw It Out the Window

Humorously

United States

SPEAKER BALANCE
CONTROL
CD
Tr. 78
Oboe   Accom.

Make up a rhyme and   sing it in time, And throw it out the win - dow!—   Make up a rhyme and

sing it in time, And throw it out the win - dow!—   The   win - dow,—   the   win - dow,—   the   sec - ond sto - ry

win - dow.—   Make up a rhyme   and   sing it in time   and throw   it out   the   win - dow!

❸ Throw It! A Round

Separated style of articulation M.M. $\quad = 108$

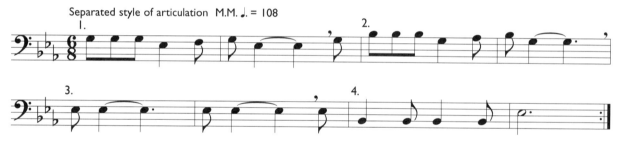

❹ Rig-A-Jig-Jig

Lightly

INTRO

United States

SPEAKER BALANCE
CONTROL
CD
Tr. 79
Horn   Accom.

As   I   was   walk - ing   down   the   street,   Down   the   street,

down   the   street,   A   pret - ty   girl   I   chanced   to   meet,   Hi - ho,   hi - ho,   hi - ho.

($\ = \.$)

Rig - a - jig - jig   and   a - way   we   go,   A - way   we   go,   A - way   we   go.

Rig - a - jig - jig   and   a - way   we   go.   Hi - ho,   hi - ho,——   hi - ho.

African Farewell (CALL AND RESPONSE)

Sierra Leone

Canon (C MAJOR SCALE CANON IN 6 PARTS)

Composer Unknown

Hallelujah (C MAJOR SCALE ROUND IN 2 PARTS)

Composer Unknown

SPECIAL PROJECT – Learn To Play *Lullaby Round* Starting on C

1 **Scale Duet** (C HARMONIC MINOR SCALE DUET)

KLEZMER – *A term that refers to a popular style of Jewish instrumetnal music.*

2 **Rozhinkes mit Mandlen (Raisins and Almonds)**

Abraham Goldfaden (1840-1906)

Smoothly with expression

To my lit-tle one's cra-dle in the night, Comes a new lit-tle goat so snow-y white. The goat will trot to the mar-ket, While moth-er her watch will keep, To bring you back rais-ins and al-monds. Sleep, my lit-tle one, sleep.

3 **A La Nanita Nana**

Spanish Lullaby

Connected style of articulation

A la-ni-ta na-na, na-ni-ta e – a, na-ni-ta e – a, mi Je-sús tie-ne sue – ño, ben-di-to se – a, ben-di-to se – a. Fuen-te-ci-lla que co-rres cla-ra y so-no-ra; rui-se-ñor de la sel-va, can-tan-do llo-ras; ca-llad mien-tras la cu-na se ba-lan-ce-a. A la-na-ni-ta na-na, na-ni-ta e – a.

4 **Ah, Poor Bird** (4–PART ROUND)

Plaintively M.M. ♩ = 104

Based on an English Round

Ah, poor bird, take your flight, Far a-bove the sor-rows of this sad night.

Accom. Tr. 30

5 **SPECIAL PROJECT** – **Return to *Cobbler, Cobbler* on Page 31 to Improvise**

FOCUS ON TEACHING
A Special Individualized Option for Spontaneous Music Making

 ●●●● **Cobbler, Cobbler**

MUSICAL DIALOGUE – A type of improvised Call and Response between two performers.

The musical dialogue, like the musical paraphrase, is an improvised conversation between two performers. A performer initiates a *Dialogue* with a 4-beat improvised *Statement* or a 4-beat improvised *Question*. A second performer responds with a 4-beat improvised *Answer*, a 4-beat improvised *Statement*, or a 4-beat improvised *Question*.

A musical **Statement** usually starts on the resting tone and always ends on the resting tone (G is the resting tone for *Cobbler, Cobbler*).

A musical **Answer** usually starts on a tone other than the resting tone and always ends on the resting tone.

A musical **Question** can begin on any tone but always ends on a tone other than the resting tone.

Direct students to employ one of the following options:

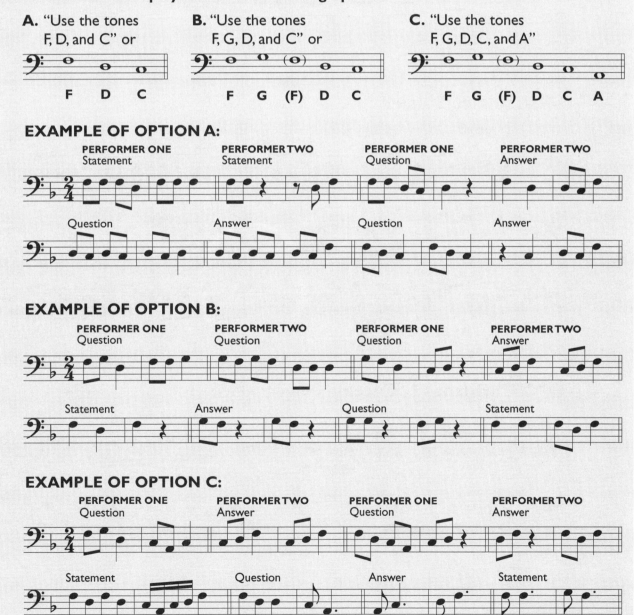

A. "Use the tones F, D, and C" or

B. "Use the tones F, G, D, and C" or

C. "Use the tones F, G, D, C, and A"

Play Along
Accom. Tr. 83

❶ **Ticky Tacky Houses** (PLAY ALONG)

With rhythmic precision

United States

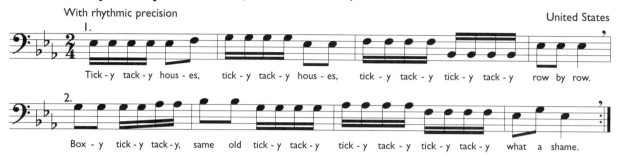

Tick-y tack-y hous-es, tick-y tack-y hous-es, tick-y tack-y tick-y tack-y row by row.

Box-y tick-y tack-y, same old tick-y tack-y tick-y tack-y tick-y tack-y what a shame.

❷ **Clocks** (3-PART ROUND)

Steady and separated M.M. ♩ = 88

Traditional

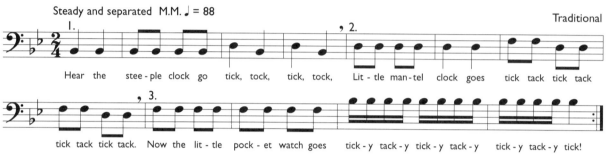

Hear the stee-ple clock go tick, tock, tick, tock, Lit-tle man-tel clock goes tick tack tick tack

tick tack tick tack. Now the lit-tle pock-et watch goes tick-y tack-y tick-y tack-y tick-y tack-y tick!

SPEAKER BALANCE
CONTROL
CD
Tr. 84
L   R
Flute Accom.

❸ **Soldier, Soldier**

Lightly
INTRO

United States

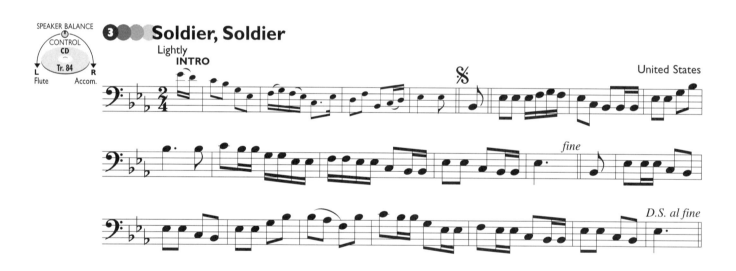

fine

D.S. al fine

❹ **Christmas Is Coming** (3-PART ROUND)

Allegro

England

PARTNER SONGS* – *Songs that may be played simultaneously to a common accompaniment.*

***When the Saints Go Marching In; This Train; and Swing Low,
Sweet Chariot are Partner Songs***

62

① The Muffin Man

Lightly

England

Oh, do you know the Muf - fin Man, the Muf - fin Man, the Muf - fin Man? Oh,

do you know the Muf - fin Man who lives on Dru - ry Lane? Oh, Lane?

FOCUS ON TEACHING
Interpreting Music Signs and Symbols

Music signs and symbols should not be interpreted literally, for example:

- $\frac{3}{4}$ may be conducted in one or three; it is open to interpretation
- $\frac{6}{8}$ may be conducted in two or six; it is open to interpretation
- $\frac{4}{4}$ may be conducted in four or two; it is open to interpretation
- $\frac{2}{4}$ ♩♩ may be performed with an even subdivision or in a swinging style; it is open to interpretation
- $\frac{2}{4}$ ♩.♩ may be performed with an even subdivision or in the style of a swinging "shuffle;" it is open to interpretation

② I Love the Mountains (5-PART ROUND)

Shuffle

England

I love the moun - tains, I love the roll - ing hills, I love the flow - ers, I love the daf - fo - dills,

I love the fire - side When all the lights are low. Boom dee ah da, boom dee ah da.

Boom dee ah da, boom dee ah. Boom dee ah da, boom dee ah da. Boom dee ah da, boom dee ah.

NEW TONE: Db 2nd

③ Jazz Waltz (SCALE TUNE)

Legato
INTRO

Based on *Scottish Lullaby*

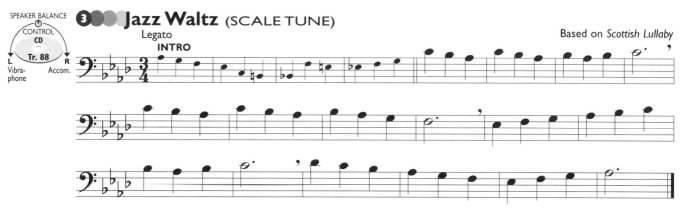

PARTNER SONGS* – *Songs that may be played simultaneously to a common accompaniment.*

This Old Man, Pawpaw Patch, Old Brass Wagon, and Bow Belinda are Partner Songs

NEW TONE: G♭ — 5th (Trombone)

REMINDER: "D♭" — 2nd (Trombone)

① College Mascots

Spirited
INTRO

United States

SPEAKER BALANCE
CONTROL
CD
Tr. 90
L — R
Trumpet   Accom.

(Drums)

Minn - e - so - ta Goph - ers,   West Vir - gin - ia 'Neers,   Col - or - a - do Buff - 'los,
Ar - i - zo - na Wild - cats,   Le - high En - gin - eers,   Ok - la - ho - ma Soon - ers,

Give your team a cheer! Mich - i - gan Wol - ver - ines,   Al - a - ba - ma Tide,   Bull - dogs, Bad - gers,   Pan - ther pride.
Give your team a cheer! Mus - ke - teers,   Vol - un - teers,   Cav - a - liers and Hogs.   Hawk - eyes, Buck - eyes,   Ducks and Frogs.

② Shenandoah

With emotion
INTRO

United States

SPEAKER BALANCE
CONTROL
CD
Tr. 91
L — R
Alto
Saxophone   Accom.

Oh,   Shen - an - doah,   I   long   to   see   you,   A -

way,   you rol - ling   riv - er,   Oh,   Shen - an - doah,   I   long   to   see   you.   A -

way,   we're bound a - way   'Cross the   wide   Mis - sou - ri.   Oh,   ri.

1.   2.

CALYPSO – A song style of Trinidad characterized by dry, witty texts and traditional steel band accompaniment.

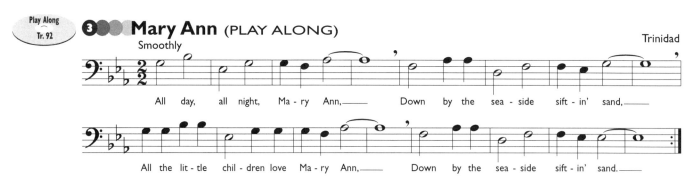

Play Along
Tr. 92

③ Mary Ann (PLAY ALONG)

Smoothly

Trinidad

All   day,   all   night,   Ma - ry   Ann,   Down   by   the   sea - side   sift - in'   sand,

All the lit - tle   chil - dren love   Ma - ry   Ann,   Down   by   the   sea - side   sift - in'   sand.

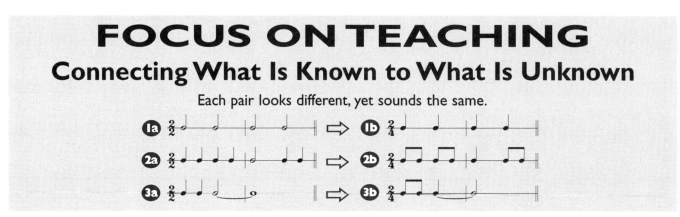

FOCUS ON TEACHING
Connecting What Is Known to What Is Unknown
Each pair looks different, yet sounds the same.

1a 2/2 ⇒ 1b 2/4

2a 2/2 ⇒ 2b 2/4

3a 2/2 ⇒ 3b 2/4

POLKA – *A lively round dance originated by Bohemian (Eastern European) peasants.*

Each pair looks different, yet sounds the same.

ENHARMONIC NOTES – *Notes that sound the same though named or spelled differently.*

Each pair looks different, yet sounds the same

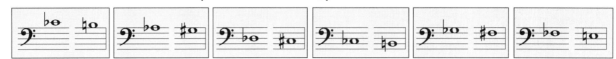

① Glow Worm

England

GEORGES BIZET (1838–1875) – *French composer; he is perhaps best known for his opera Carmen.*

TRIPLET – *Three notes of equal rhythmic value grouped together with a "3" over or under them.*

HEMIOLA – *Literally, three against two. In 4 time signature, a hemiola is represented by three quarter notes performed evenly during the same duration as 2 quarter notes.*

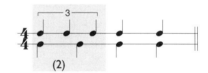

② Habanera (FROM THE OPERA CARMEN)

Georges Bizet

③ Chromatic Scale

REMINDER: "E♭" 3rd

1 Saint Anthony Chorale (MELODY – FOR SOLO OR ENSEMBLE PERFORMANCE)

With expression

Franz Joseph Haydn

2 Saint Anthony Chorale (HARMONY PART 1 – FOR DUET, TRIO, OR ENSEMBLE PERFORMANCE)

3 Saint Anthony Chorale (HARMONY PART 2 – FOR DUET, TRIO, OR ENSEMBLE PERFORMANCE)

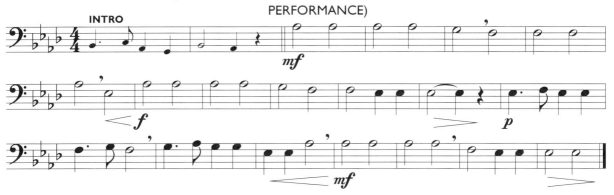

4 Saint Anthony Chorale (BASS PART)

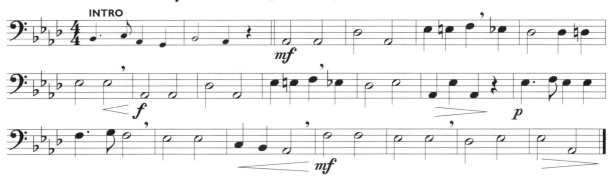

MERENGUE – A distinct dance music tradition of Haiti in duple meter.

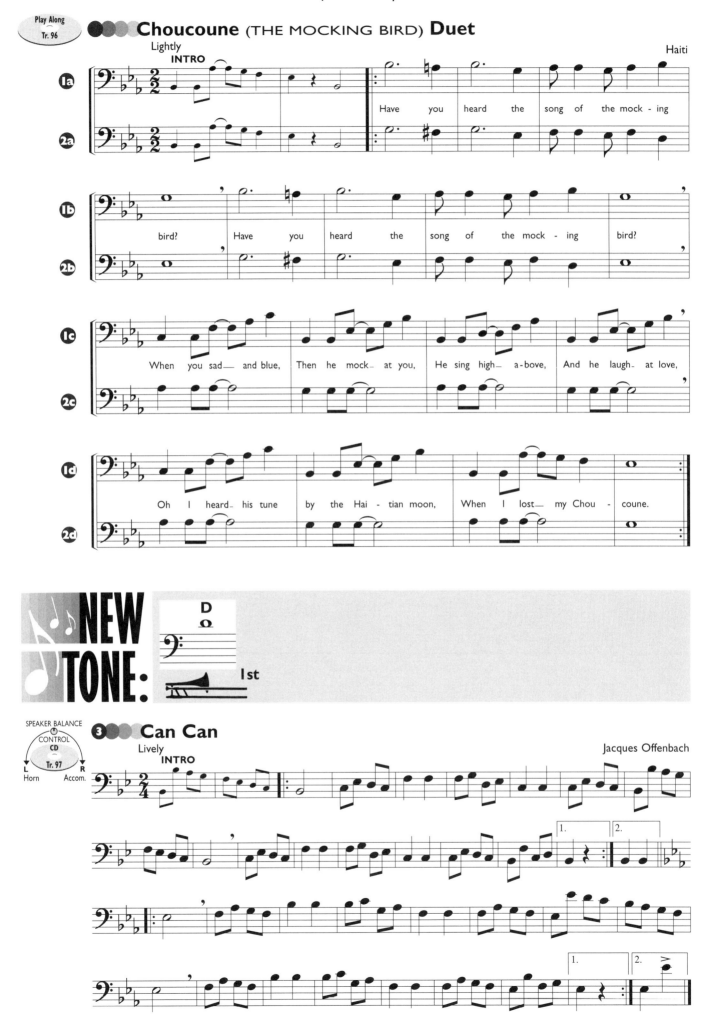

Choucoune (THE MOCKING BIRD) **Duet**

Haiti

Have you heard the song of the mock - ing
bird? Have you heard the song of the mock - ing bird?
When you sad— and blue, Then he mock at you, He sing high— a-bove, And he laugh— at love,
Oh I heard— his tune by the Hai - tian moon, When I lost— my Chou - coune.

NEW TONE: D 1st

Can Can

Jacques Offenbach

AURAL TRANSPOSITION
A Musical Assessment of "By Ear" Playing Technique[1]

AMERICA

Samuel Francis Smith
Henry Carey

Expressively

Assignment #1: Learn to play this fragment of *America* starting on E♭, A♭, D♭, G♭, and C.

Assignment #2: Learn to play the entire song starting on E♭, A♭, D♭, G♭, and C.

THOU, POOR BIRD

Smoothly   Round

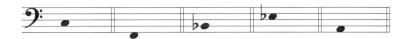

Assignment: Learn to play *Thou, Poor Bird* starting on C, F, B♭, E♭, and A.

MARY ANN

With spirit   Calypso Song

Assignment: Learn to play this fragment of *Mary Ann* starting on G, G, F, B♭, and E.

[1]Excerpts taken from *Studies in Aural Transposition* (Froseth, M442). www.giamusic.com

SCALE ROUNDS IN MAJOR
A Musical Assessment of Technical Skill

SCALE ROUNDS IN MINOR
A Musical Assessment of Technical Skill

#9 - 4-Part Round in C Natural Minor

#10 - 4-Part Round in A Natural Minor

#11 - 4-Part Round in D Natural Minor

#12 - 4-Part Round in Bb Natural Minor

#13 - Transpose #12 above to G Natural Minor

#14 - 4-Part Round in A Harmonic Minor

#15 - 4-Part Round in Bb Harmonic Minor

#16 - 4-Part Round in D Harmonic Minor

#17 - Transpose #16 above to G Harmonic Minor

72

RESOURCES FOR SELF-DIRECTED PROFESSIONAL DEVELOPMENT

Movement to Music Skills

• A prerequisite to the development of music listening, reading, writing, performance, and conducting skills

• A form of aesthetic experience

Resource: Froseth, James O., Albert Blaser, and Phyllis Weikart. *Music for Movement*. Book and compact disc. Chicago: G.I.A., 1993. M-189BKCD

Resource: Froseth, James O. *Move to the Sound of World Music*. Compact disc. Chicago: G.I.A., 2006. CD-668

Rhythmic Verbal Association Skills (Phonetic Rhythmic Syllables – Froseth/Blaser)

• A vocal language that codifies rhythm

• A way to think intelligently about rhythmic patterns that you hear

• A means to musically dictate rhythm

Resource: Froseth, James O., and Albert Blaser. *MLR Verbal Association Skills Program Part One: Rhythm*. Compact disc. Chicago: G.I.A., 1999. MLR-378CD

Resource: Froseth, James O. *Rhythmic Flashcards Set One*. Includes compact disc. Chicago: G.I.A., 1998. MLR-421

Melodic Verbal Association Skills (Solfége - Kodaly Movable Do)

• A vocal language that codifies melody and harmony

• A way to think intelligently about melodic patterns and harmonic progressions that you hear

• A means to musically dictate melody and harmony

Resource: Froseth, James O., and Albert Blaser. *MLR Verbal Association Skills Program Part Two: Melody (Solfége)*. Compact disc. Chicago: G.I.A., 1999. MLR-379CD

Resource: Froseth, James O. *Melodic Flashcards for Recorder*. Includes compact disc. Chicago: G.I.A., 1998. MLR-489

Melodic and Harmonic Ear-to-Hand Coordination Skills ("By Ear")

• The means to transfer what is heard, recalled, or imagined to instrumental performance "by ear" without the aid of music notation

• A foundation skill for music memorization

• A foundation skill for music modeling

• A foundation skill for music improvisation

• A means to musically dictate rhythm, melody, and harmony

Resource: Froseth, James O. *Performance-Based Ear Training: Studies in Aural Transposition.* Book. Chicago: G.I.A., 1996. MLR-442

Resource: Froseth, James O. *Performance-Based Ear Training: Performing Patterns and Scales 'Round the Circle'.* Book and compact disc. Chicago: G.I.A., 1994. M-424/425/426/427/428/429/431/432/433/434 (books) AND M-451 (compact disc)

Resource: Froseth, James O. *MLR Melodic Ear-to-Hand Skills Program.* Audio cassettes. Chicago: G.I.A., 1985. MLR-408

Resource: Froseth, James O. *MLR Harmonic Ear-to-Hand Skills Program.* Audio cassettes. Chicago: G.I.A., 1985. MLR-400

Resource: Froseth, James O. *MLR Harmonizing Melodies Ear-to-Hand Skills Program.* Audio cassettes. Chicago: G.I.A., 1985. MLR-399

Resource: Froseth, James O., and Albert Blaser. *Do It! Improvise!* Compact disc and booklet. Chicago: G.I.A., 1994. MLR-422

Resource: Froseth, James O., and David Froseth. *Do It! Improvise II! In All the Modes.* Compact disc and booklet. Chicago: G.I.A., 1995. MLR-424CD

Aural and Visual Diagnostic Skills

• The essential prerequisite to remediating individual instrumental performance problems

• A means for diagnosing and correcting ensemble performance problems

Resource: Froseth, James O., and Michael T. Hopkins. *Visual Diagnostic Skills Program.* CD-ROM. Chicago: G.I.A., 2004. M536 (brass) and M537 (woodwinds)

Resource: Grunow, Richard F., and James O. Froseth. *MLR Instrumental Score Reading Program.* Workbook and compact discs. Chicago: G.I.A., 1982. G-2313 (workbook) and G-2313CD (compact discs)

Teacher Self-Assessment Skills

• The essential means to become "aware of what you are unaware of" in the classroom, studio, and rehearsal hall

• The means to take control of your professional development in the classroom, studio, and rehearsal hall

Resource: Froseth, James O., and Molly A. Weaver. *Music Teacher Self-Assessment: A Diagnostic Tool for Professional Development.* Videocassette and manual. Chicago: G.I.A., 1996. MLR-444

www.giamusic.com

CHART OF TROMBONE HAND SLIDE POSITIONS

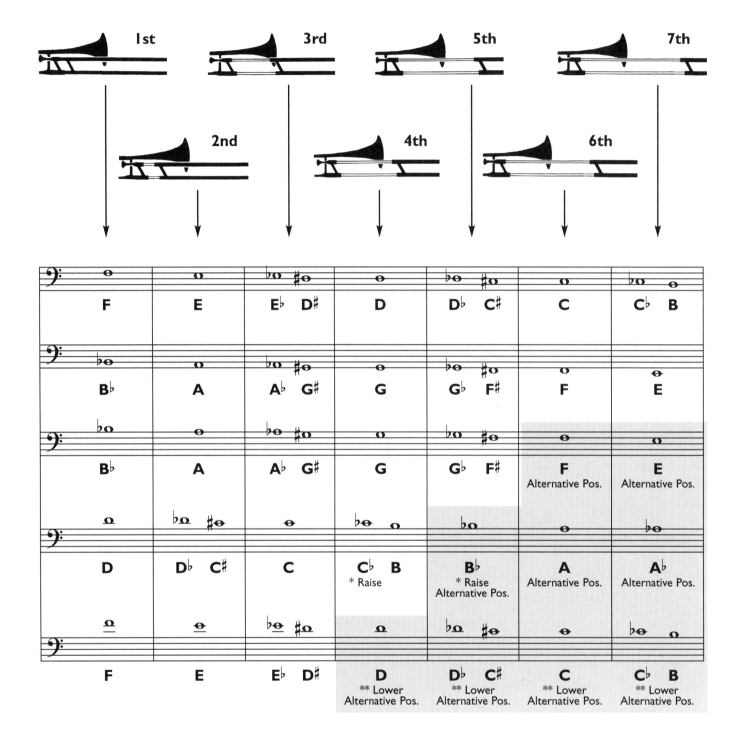

*When the word "Raise" appears below a note, adjust the slide position *inward* slightly to tune the note.

**When the word "Lower" appears below a note, adjust the slide position *outward* slightly to tune the note.